Walking in Power, Love, and Discipline

KAY ARTHUR
DAVID LAWSON
BOB VEREEN

HARVEST HOUSE PUBLISHERS
EUGENE, OREGON

All Scripture quotations in this book are taken from the New American Standard Bible®, © 1960, 1962, 1963, 1968, 1971, 1972, 1973, 1975, 1977, 1995 by The Lockman Foundation. Used by permission.

Except where otherwise indicated, all maps and charts in this book, as well as the "How to Get Started" portion of the introductory material, have been adapted and condensed from *The New Inductive Study Bible,* Copyright © 2000 by Precept Ministries International.

Cover by Koechel Peterson & Associates, Inc., Minneapolis, Minnesota

The New Inductive Study Series
WALKING IN POWER, LOVE, AND DISCIPLINE

Copyright © 2002 by Precept Ministries International
Published by Harvest House Publishers
Eugene, Oregon 97402
www.harvesthousepublishers.com

Library of Congress Cataloging-in-Publication Data
Arthur, Kay, 1933–
      Walking in Power, Love, and Discipline / Kay Arthur, Bob Vereen, David Lawson.
         p. cm. — (The new inductive study series)
      ISBN 978-0-7369-0811-5 (pbk.)
      ISBN 978-0-7369-3669-9 (eBook)
      1. Bible. N.T. Pastoral Epistles— Study and teaching.   I. Vereen, Bob.
   II. Lawson, David.   III. Title.
   BS2735.5 .A78 2000
   227'.830071— dc21   99-057269
                                                                CIP

All rights reserved. No part of this publication may be reproduced, stored in a retrieval system, or transmitted in any form or by any means—electronic, mechanical, digital, photocopy, recording, or any other—except for brief quotations in printed reviews, without the prior permission of the publisher.

Printed in the United States of America.

20 21 22 23 / BP-VS / 18 17 16

CONTENTS

What Am I Doing? 5

How to Get Started... 7

Walking in the Truth. 15

1 TIMOTHY
Introduction to 1 Timothy. 18

Week One
What Is the Truth? 19

Week Two
Living the Truth in the Church 27

Week Three
The Truth About Qualifications
    for Leadership. 35

Week Four
The Truth Is, God Does Care How I Act. 41

Week Five
The Truth About Elders
    and Money 47

2 TIMOTHY
Introduction to 2 Timothy. 54

Week One
Inheriting a Fortune 55

Week Two
To Heaven or to Hell? That's the Question . . . 65

Week Three
   Can a Real Child of God Be Recognized?..... 75

Week Four
   Are We Living in the Last Days?............ 87

Week Five
   What Will They Say About You
      When You're Gone? 99

TITUS
Introduction to Titus 108

Week One
   What Are the Requirements
      for a Godly Leader?.................. 109

Week Two
   What Does Godliness Look Like in Me? 115

Week Three
   What Makes You Different? 123

   Notes 131

WHAT AM I DOING?

You are about to begin a study that will revolutionize not only your approach to the Word of God, but also your understanding and comprehension of the Word. This is the consistent testimony of those who are using this series.

The New Inductive Study Series is the first series of its kind in that it is a 15- to 25-minute daily study that takes you systematically through the Bible, book by book, teaching you to observe the text and see for yourself what it says. The more you learn to observe the text carefully and to familiarize yourself with the context in which specific texts are presented, the closer you will come to an accurate and unbiased interpretation of God's Word. This, in turn, will help you to apply the truth of God's Word correctly and to find yourself transformed in the process.

As you go through this series, remember that it is an inductive survey of the various books of the Bible. The purpose of this series is to help you get a comprehensive overview of the whole counsel of God so that you will be better able to let Scripture interpret Scripture and to understand truth in the context of the Bible, book by book and in its entirety.

If you desire to expand and sharpen your study skills, we would like to recommend two things. One, purchase the book *How to Study Your Bible* by Kay Arthur. Two, attend a Precept Ministries Institute of Training.

The Institutes are conducted throughout the United States, Canada, and in a number of other countries. You can attend classes of various lengths—from one to five days, depending on the courses you elect to take. Whatever your choices, you will join the thousands of people who are absolutely awed at the way God has enriched their relationship with Him and deepened their understanding of His Word. For more information on the Precept Ministries Institute of Training, call our Customer Service Representatives at (800) 763-8280, visit our website at www.precept.org, or fill out and mail the response card at the back of this book.

We don't know if you have ever used one of the books in our New Inductive Study Series before, so let us acknowledge that reading directions is sometimes difficult and hardly ever enjoyable. Most often, you just want to get started. Only if all else fails are you ready to tackle the instructions! We understand—we're not into details either. But read "How to Get Started" before you begin. This is a vital part of getting started on the right foot. The pages are few...and they will help you immensely.

HOW TO GET STARTED...

FIRST

As you study the books of 1 and 2 Timothy and Titus, you will need four things in addition to this book:

1. A Bible that you are willing to mark in. Marking is essential because it is an integral part of the learning process and will help you remember and retain what you learned. An ideal Bible for this purpose is *The New Inductive Study Bible (NISB)*. The *NISB*, available in the New American Standard Version comes in a single-column text format with larger, easy-to-read type, and is ideal for marking. The page margins are wide and blank for note-taking.

The *NISB* is unique among all study Bibles in that it has instructions for studying each book of the Bible, but it does not contain any commentary on the text. The *NISB* isn't compiled from any particular theological stance since its purpose is to teach you how to discern truth for yourself through the inductive method of study. Inductive Bible study simply means that the Bible itself is the primary source for study. (The various charts and maps that you will find in this study guide are taken from the *NISB*.) Whatever Bible you use, just know you will need to mark in it, which brings us to the second item you will need.

2. A fine-point, four-color ballpoint pen or various colored fine-point pens (such as Micron pens) for writing in

your Bible. The Micron pens are best for this purpose. Office supply stores should have these.

3. Colored pencils or an eight-color Pentel pencil.

4. A composition notebook or loose-leaf notebook for working on your assignments and recording your insights.

SECOND

1. As you study this book, you'll find specific instructions for each day's study. The study should take you between 15 and 25 minutes a day. However, just know that the more time you can give to this study, the greater the spiritual dividends, the greater your intimacy with the Word of God and the God of the Word. If you are doing this study within the framework of a class and you find the lessons too heavy, simply do what you can. To do a little is better than to do nothing. Don't be an all-or-nothing person when it comes to Bible study.

As a word of warning, you need to be aware that any time you get into the Word of God, you enter into more intensive warfare with the devil (our enemy). Why? Every piece of the Christian's armor is related to the Word of God. And the enemy doesn't want you prepared for battle. Thus, the warfare! Remember that our one and only offensive weapon is the sword of the Spirit, which is the Word of God, and it is enough to fell the enemy.

To study or not to study is a matter of choice first, discipline second. It's a matter of the heart. On what or whom are you setting your heart? Get armed for war! And remember, victory is certain.

2. As you read each chapter, train yourself to think through the content of the text by asking the "5 W's and an H": who, what, when, where, why, and how. Posing questions like these and searching out the answers help you see

exactly what the Word of God is saying. When you interrogate the text with the 5 W's and an H, you ask questions like these:

a. **Who** are the main characters?

b. **What** is the chapter about?

c. **When** does this event or teaching take place?

d. **Where** does this occur?

e. **Why** is this being done or said?

f. **How** did this happen?

3. The "when" of events or teachings is very important and should be marked in an easily recognizable way in your Bible. We do this by putting a clock (like the one shown here) in the margin of our Bibles beside the verse where the time phrase occurs. Or you may want to underline references to time in one specific color. As a reminder, note on your key-word bookmark (which is explained next in this section) how you are going to mark time references in each chapter.

4. You will be told about certain key words that you should mark throughout this study. This is the purpose of the colored pencils and the colored pen. While this may seem a little time-consuming, you will discover that it is a valuable learning tool. If you will develop the habit of marking your Bible, you will find it will make a significant difference in the effectiveness of your study and in how much you retain as a result of your study.

A **key word** is an important word that is used by the author repeatedly in order to convey his message to his reader. Certain key words will show up throughout the book, while other key words will be concentrated in specific chapters or segments of the book. When you mark a key word, you should also mark its synonyms (words that have the same meaning in a particular context) and any pronouns (*he, his, she, her, it, we, they, us, our, you, their, them*) in the same way you have marked the key word. Because some people have requested them, we will give you various ideas and suggestions in your daily assignments for how you can mark different key words.

Marking words for easy identification can be done by colors, symbols, or a combination of colors and symbols. However, colors are easier to distinguish than symbols. If you use symbols, we suggest you keep them very simple. For example, one of the key words in 1 Timothy is *law.* You could draw a tablet like this over law and color it black. If a symbol is used in marking a key word, it is best for the symbol to somehow convey the meaning of the word.

As you begin this new venture, we recommend that you devise a color-coding system for marking key words that you decide to mark throughout your Bible. Then, when you glance at the pages of your Bible, you will have instant recognition of the words.

In marking the members of the Godhead (which we do not always mark), we use a triangle to represent the Father. We then color it yellow. Then, playing off the triangle, we mark the Son this way: Jesus , and the Holy Spirit this way: Spirit . We find that when you mark every reference to God and Jesus, your Bible becomes cluttered. However, since the Spirit is mentioned less and because many people do not have a thorough biblical understanding of the Holy Spirit, it is good to mark all the references to the Spirit of God.

When you start marking key words, it is easy to forget how you are marking them. Therefore, we recommend that you list the key words on an index card and use different symbols and/or colors to mark each word. Mark the words in the way you plan to mark each in the Bible text, and then use the card as a bookmark. Make one bookmark for words you are marking throughout your Bible, and a different one for any specific book of the Bible you are studying. Or record your marking system for the words you plan to mark throughout your Bible on a blank page in your Bible.

5. Because locations are important in Epistles and they tell you "where," you will find it helpful to mark locations in a distinguishable way in your study. Try double underlining every reference to a location in green (grass and trees are green!). We suggest that you make a note on your keyword bookmark to mark locations.

6. Charts called 1 TIMOTHY AT A GLANCE, 2 TIMOTHY AT A GLANCE, and TITUS AT A GLANCE are located at the end of each section. When you complete your study of each chapter of these books, record the main theme of that chapter on the appropriate chart. A chapter theme is a brief description or summary of the main theme or predominant subject, teaching, or event covered in that chapter.

When stating chapter themes, it is best to use words found within the text itself and to be as brief as possible. Make sure that you do them in such a way as to distinguish one chapter from another. Doing this will help you to remember what each chapter is about. In addition, it will provide you with a ready reference if you desire to find something in the book rather quickly and without a lot of page turning.

If you develop the habit of filling out the AT A GLANCE charts as you progress through the study, you will have a complete synopsis of the book when you finish. If you have a *New Inductive Study Bible,* you will find the same charts in your Bible. If you record your chapter themes on the charts in your Bible and on the designated line at the head of each chapter in the text, you'll always have a quick synopsis of the chapter and the book.

7. Begin your study with prayer. Don't start without it. Why? Well, although you are doing your part to handle the Word of God accurately, remember that the Bible is a divinely inspired book. The words you are reading are absolute truth, given to you by God so that you can know Him and His ways more intimately. These truths are divinely understood.

> For to us God revealed them through the Spirit;
> for the Spirit searches all things, even the depths
> of God. For who among men knows the thoughts
> of a man except the spirit of the man which is in
> him? Even so the thoughts of God no one knows
> except the Spirit of God (1 Corinthians 2:10,11).

This is why you need to pray. Simply tell God you want to understand His Word so you can live accordingly. Nothing pleases Him more than obedience—honoring Him as God—as you are about to see.

8. Each day, when you finish your lesson, take some time to think about what you read, what you saw with your own eyes. Ask your heavenly Father how you can apply these insights, principles, precepts, and commands to your own life. At times, depending on how God speaks to you through His Word, you might want to record these "Lessons for Life" in the margin of your Bible next to the text you have studied. Simply put "LFL" in the margin of your Bible; then, as briefly as possible, record the lesson for

life that you want to remember. You can also make the note "LFL" on your key word bookmark as a reminder to look for these when you study. You will find them encouraging (and sometimes convicting) when you come across them again. They will be a reminder of what God has shown you from His Word.

THIRD

This study is designed so that you have an assignment for every day of the week. This puts you where you should be—in the Word of God on a daily basis, grasping, systematizing, and utilizing truth. It's revolutionary!

If you will do your study daily, you will find it more profitable than doing a week's study in one sitting. Pacing yourself this way allows time for thinking through what you learn on a daily basis. However, whatever it takes to get it done, do it!

The seventh day of each week has several features that differ from the other six days. These features are designed to aid in one-on-one discipleship, group discussions, and Sunday school classes. However, they are also profitable even if you are studying this book by yourself.

The "seventh" day is whatever day in the week you choose to think about and/or discuss your week's study. On this day, you will find a verse or two to memorize and thus STORE IN YOUR HEART. This will help you focus on a major truth or truths covered in your study that week.

To assist those using the material for discipleship, family devotions, or in a Sunday school class or a group Bible study, there are QUESTIONS FOR DISCUSSION OR INDIVIDUAL STUDY. Whatever your situation, seeking to answer these questions will help you reason through some key issues in the study.

If you are using the study in a group setting, make sure the answers given are supported from the Bible text itself. This practice will help ensure that you are handling the Word of God accurately. As you learn to see what the text says, you will find that the Bible explains itself.

Always examine your insights by carefully observing the text to see what it *says.* Then, before you decide what the passage of Scripture *means,* make sure you interpret it in the light of its context. Context is what goes with the text...the Scriptures preceding and following what is written. Scripture will never contradict Scripture. If a Scripture passage ever seems to contradict the rest of the Word of God, you can be certain that something is being taken out of context. If you come to a passage that is difficult to understand, reserve your interpretations for a time when you can study the passage in greater depth.

Your discussion time should cause you to see how to apply these truths to your own life. What are you now going to embrace as truth? How are you going to order your life? Are you going to not only know these truths but also live accordingly?

The purpose of a Thought for the Week is to help you apply what you've learned. We've done this for your edification. In this, a little of our theology will inevitably come to the surface; however, we don't ask that you always agree with us. Rather, think through what is said in light of the context of the Word of God. You can determine how valuable it is.

Remember, books in the New Inductive Study Series are survey courses. If you want to do a more in-depth study of a particular book of the Bible, we suggest you do a Precept Upon Precept Bible Study Course on that book. The Precept studies are awesome but require five hours of personal study a week.

WALKING IN THE TRUTH

What could be gained by a study of the personal letters of a first-century missionary to his two most trusted disciples? In this case, a knowledge of the truth. Paul wrote almost half of the New Testament, but only four of his letters are to individuals. Three—the three we will study together for the next 13 weeks—are to his primary lieutenants, Titus and Timothy. These were men that he trained to be elders in the church. He loved them as if they were his own sons. They served him as if he was their father. Historically, these have been called the "Pastoral Epistles" since these men were serving as pastors. Although these are personal letters to the local pastors, the truth they contain is eternal; it is universal. What Paul shares goes beyond the bounds of personal remarks to define sound doctrine (real truth) and sound discipline (right behavior) for the church of the ages.

Study with us for the next 13 weeks, and we will help you discover the truth and how to live.

1 TIMOTHY

INTRODUCTION TO 1 TIMOTHY

Thirty years of labor for the gospel had taken its toll on Paul. His body bore the brand-marks of a servant of Jesus Christ. However, the intensity of his sufferings never changed the intensity of his love and concern for the churches which were etched on his heart.

One of these churches was Ephesus. Timothy, his faithful disciple, was pastoring that strategically important church. Possibly concerned that he might be delayed and that Timothy might need something in writing to set before others as an ever-present reminder, Paul took quill and ink, spread out the parchment, and wrote his first letter to his son in the faith. This letter would become a legacy for the church, defining both sound doctrine (truth), and sound discipline (right behavior). It was about A.D. 62.

WHAT IS THE TRUTH?

ຕາຕາຕາ

DAY ONE

Before we begin our study, be sure to read the "How to Get Started" section beginning on page 7. This information will make your study easier and more exciting.

To understand *what* the apostle Paul means by what he says, it is very helpful to know *why* he is writing. Sometimes he states his purposes very clearly; sometimes he only hints. Today we will begin the process of determining the context of 1 Timothy by looking at the first three chapters. Read 1 Timothy 1–3. Since this is a letter, read it as if you had just received it in the mail. See if you can discover why he is writing and why he left Timothy in Ephesus. The answers to these two questions will help us establish the context of the letter and understand why he says what he does. Just read straight through—don't get distracted by difficult passages now. We will get answers in due time. Simply familiarize yourself with the letter.

The word *context* comes from a Latin word meaning "to weave together." Before we can understand a passage, we must see what it is woven together with. In other words, we need to see what is talked about before it and after it.

Reading through the book will help you see the big picture and then make it easier to see the context of each passage.

Before you start, pray. Always ask the Father for guidance when you are studying His Book. Enjoy.

DAY TWO

Did you discover Paul's purpose? Just in case you missed it, he tells us why he left Timothy in Ephesus in 1:3, and why he is writing in 3:14,15. Read chapters 4–6 to familiarize yourself with the rest of this letter. When you finish, record Paul's purpose in writing and his purpose in leaving Timothy in Ephesus on your AT A GLANCE chart, page 52. These two purposes will help us interpret the difficult passages by giving us a context from which to work.

DAY THREE

Today focus your attention on 1 Timothy 1. Mark every reference to *doctrines*[1] and any synonyms such as *instruction*[2] or *sound teaching*.[3] Continue to mark these words throughout your study of 1 Timothy. The word doctrine simply means "a teaching." You will notice that Paul describes sound and unsound doctrine. Start a list in your notebook of what you learn about each one. Title your lists "Sound Doctrine" and "Unsound Doctrine," respectively. On your list identify what strange doctrine looks like according to verse 4. Also, under "Sound Doctrine," record the goal of our instruction according to verse 5. In the next weeks, you will add to this list as you see the word *doctrine* or its synonyms in 1 Timothy.

Read 1 Timothy 1:1-11 again and mark every reference to *law*. I draw a black tablet like this ⬛ which represents two tablets of stone. When you finish, list everything you learn about the law. For example, in verse 8 we learn "the Law is good if one uses it lawfully." Did you notice in verse 9 who the law is for and who it isn't for?

DAY FOUR

The best interpreter of Scripture is Scripture. Many times looking at other passages of Scripture will help give understanding to the passage you are studying. This is called cross-referencing. Read Galatians 3:23-29 and mark every reference to *law* and *faith*. In your notebook, list what you learn about each one. Also, take a few minutes to reflect on what you have learned about sound doctrine. According to 1 Timothy 1:5, what is the goal of sound doctrine or instruction?

DAY FIVE

When we study the Bible, it is always important to pay close attention to what we learn about Jesus Christ. Today read 1 Timothy 1 and Galatians 3:23-29 again. In both passages mark every reference to *Jesus Christ* and the pronouns which refer to Him. Pay close attention to 1 Timothy 1:12-17. This is the first doctrinal passage in this letter where the gospel is presented. You don't want to miss this. When you finish, start a list in your notebook of everything you learn about Jesus Christ. To mark *Christ*, I use the same symbol and color shown in the "How to Get Started" section, but you are free to develop any marking system which suits you.

DAY SIX

To keep yourself in context, read 1 Timothy 1 today. As you do, mark each reference to *Timothy*. When you finish, list what you learn about Timothy's responsibilities. In other words, what is Timothy charged to do?

Now read 1 Timothy 4:6. How does this compare with what you have learned in chapter 1 about Timothy's responsibilities?

I know by now you must be curious about this man Timothy. You will learn more about him when you study 2 Timothy, but for now let me say that he was Paul's most trusted disciple. Paul even described Timothy as a man of kindred spirit. Enough for now—you will see more later.

When you finish, record what chapter 1 is about (the main idea or theme) in as few words as possible on your AT A GLANCE chart on page 52.

DAY SEVEN

 Store in your heart: 1 Timothy 1:5.
Read and discuss: 1 Timothy 1.

QUESTIONS FOR DISCUSSION OR INDIVIDUAL STUDY

∾ What was Paul's purpose in writing this letter to Timothy? Why did he leave Timothy in Ephesus? Which of these purposes relates to knowing the truth or knowing sound doctrine? Which relates to living the truth or walking in sound discipline?

∾ Discuss the characteristics of the strange doctrines against which Paul warns Timothy. What is the result of these unsound teachings?

∾ What did you learn about the law from 1 Timothy? What did you learn about the law from Galatians? What is the purpose of the law? Who is the law for? What is the relationship of the law to salvation?

∾ Once you come to know Christ, what relationship do you have with the law? What did you learn about Jesus Christ this week? What difference should it make in your life?

∾ In 1 Timothy 1:18, Paul says, "This command I entrust to you...." What command is he talking about? What was the last command he gave Timothy in chapter 1? In your communication of the Word of God, are you careful to adhere to sound teaching? What is the goal of sound doctrine? Can you adhere to sound teaching if you don't know what the Bible says?

THOUGHT FOR THE WEEK

Our focus this week has been on knowing the truth, on knowing sound doctrine. Paul left Timothy in Ephesus in order that he might instruct certain men not to teach strange doctrines. As you study this letter, you need to pay close attention to the truth being presented. The false doctrines Timothy faced are still around in religion today. Do you know the truth well enough to recognize strange doctrine when you hear it? It is vital that you know what God has said instead of simply what man has said about God.

Being dependent on man places you in the dangerous position of being susceptible to strange doctrines.

What is strange doctrine? We may not know everything Timothy faced, but part of the false teaching had to do with the law. This was probably the law of Moses as interpreted by the Pharisees. They taught that to get into a right relationship with God one had to keep the law. You studied that this week. Are you made right with God by keeping rules and regulations? No, of course not. You have seen in Galatians 3:24 that we are justified (put in right relationship with God) by faith. In 1 Timothy 1:15 you saw that Jesus came into the world to save sinners (those who have violated God's law, not those who have kept it).

The point Paul is making in both of these passages is that you are saved by faith, not by keeping some external set of rules or regulations. To come into a relationship with God, we must first recognize that we have sinned against Him. Paul talks about this in relationship to himself in chapter 1, verses 12-17. We then must surrender our will to God's. This is what it means to call Him Lord. Did you notice that there is no mention of keeping any rules or regulations? You enter into this relationship by placing your faith, your trust, in what Christ has done for you.

What is sound doctrine? You saw some of the answer in chapter 1:12-17. Christ came into the world to save sinners. In Him is found mercy, grace, faith, and love. The goal of sound doctrine is love from a pure heart, a good conscience, and a sincere faith. It is enough for this week; we will see more in chapter 2.

If I am not under the law, can I live any way I want? Good question. This week we focused on knowing the truth. Later we will talk about living the truth (in chapters 4, 5, and 6).

Now for the question I know you have been asking: What about Alexander and Hymenaeus? They were apparently teachers of strange doctrine. Paul's use of the phrase "handed over to Satan" means that he excommunicated them from the church. The early church believed that unscriptural teaching was so dangerous that anyone found engaging in it was excommunicated. What an idea! You will see these two men mentioned in 2 Timothy when you do the next study.

LIVING THE TRUTH IN THE CHURCH

DAY ONE

Today read 1 Timothy 3:14,15 to remind yourself of Paul's purpose in writing. Keep this purpose in mind this week as you study because it will help with some passages we will study later. Remember, we saw last week that Paul's purpose in leaving Timothy at Ephesus involved the need for sound doctrine. In verse 1 of chapter 2 you will see a shift in subjects. His purpose in writing this passage centers around sound behavior.

Now read 1 Timothy 2:1-8. In your notebook list what you learn about prayer from this passage. The simplest way to do this is to question the text as you read. Ask yourself who, what, when, where, why, and how questions. For example, in verse 1 Paul says, "I urge that entreaties and prayers, petitions and thanksgivings, be made on behalf of all men." After reading this, the logical questions are:

What? (prayers, entreaties, petitions, and thanksgivings)

For whom? (on behalf of all men)

Do you have the idea? Now see what you can learn about prayer.

DAY TWO

What does Paul want to take place in church? Prayer. Read 1 Timothy 2:1-8 again. This time mark the references to *God* and *Christ*. Also mark any pronouns that refer to either of them. Mark *Christ* the same way you did last week in chapter 1. If you are not sure how to mark *God*, refer to the "How to Get Started" section. When you finish, add to your list in your notebook what you learn about Jesus Christ and begin a list on what you learn about God. This is the second great doctrinal passage in this letter.

Did you notice the phrase "God our Savior"? This is a very unusual title for God in the Bible. It is used six times in the Old Testament and seven times in the New Testament. In 1 Timothy it is used in 1:1; 2:3; and 4:10. You will see it three more times when you do the Titus study, so watch for it there.

DAY THREE

The remainder of this week we will focus on 1 Timothy 2:8-15. This passage is a controversial one, but we will take one step at a time. Before we start, let me ask you a question: What is Paul's purpose in writing? He wants you to know how to conduct yourself where? Remember 1 Timothy 3:14,15?

Today read 1 Timothy 2:8-15. Then list in your notebook how a woman is to adorn herself and how she is not to adorn herself. When you finish, cross-reference this passage with 1 Peter 3:1-6. Add to your notebook any new insights you gain.

If you have time, read Song of Solomon 1:9-11 and Genesis 24:10-30,53. Watch for references to jewelry, especially to gold.

Is Paul forbidding a woman to wear jewelry? Or is God's emphasis on the inward adornment versus the outward appearance? From these references it seems that God is more concerned about the attitude of the heart than He is about our outward appearance.

DAY FOUR

Today read 1 Timothy 2:8-15 again. As you do, keep in mind Paul's purpose in writing as he has stated in 3:14,15. List in your notebook what a woman is to do and what she is not allowed to do and why. Where is this pattern of behavior to be implemented? You must keep everything in context—don't jump to conclusions. Just let the text say what the text says. We're not finished yet!

Don't forget to mark the word *instruction*[4] in 2:11.

DAY FIVE

Today let's look at 1 Corinthians 14:26-40, another passage of Scripture that discusses order in the public worship service. Read it carefully and watch as Paul establishes a context. Don't let yourself become distracted by the spiritual gifts that are mentioned. They are for another study, for another time. List in your notebook the restrictions Paul places on the worship service. What does Paul say concerning the use of tongues in the worship service, the use of prophecy in the worship service, and women speaking in church? Remember, we are focusing on the role of women in the church.

DAY SIX

In 1 Timothy 2:8-15 is Paul saying that women cannot teach in a church building? Is he saying women cannot teach at all? What about Sunday school? Is a woman never allowed to teach her husband? What about other men? The answers to these questions must come from Scripture, not from our opinions or from the traditions of men. You cannot depend on what you have heard but only on what God has said.

Let's cross-reference two passages. Read Acts 18:24-28. Watch for the names of the two people who instructed Apollos. Also read Titus 2:1-5. Notice the duties of the older women. When you finish, record the main theme of chapter 2 on the AT A GLANCE chart on page 52. Then take a moment to meditate on what you have learned.

DAY SEVEN

 Store in your heart: 1 Timothy 2:5,6.
Read and discuss: 1 Timothy 1:3,4; 2:1-15; 3:14,15.

QUESTIONS FOR DISCUSSION OR INDIVIDUAL STUDY

∾ Paul has shown us two reasons for writing this letter. What are they? How does the second purpose he gave help explain chapter 2:1-7?

∾ Who are we to pray for? Do you pray regularly for the president and those in authority over you? How can we incorporate prayer for our authorities into our worship service? If I am to be praying for "all who are in authority," should this change my political humor? My complaining? Who else am I to pray for besides those in authority and the king (or in our case, the president)?

∾ What did you learn about God this week? What does God desire? What are you personally doing to fulfill God's desire?

∾ What did you learn about Christ this week? What is a mediator? Who is our mediator? How is mediating like prayer? What does it mean to you that Jesus is mediating on your behalf before the Father?

∾ According to Paul, how is a woman to adorn herself? Why? Is God against gold and pearls? Would silver and platinum be better? Ladies, how are you adorning yourselves? On what are you focused? Parents, are you teaching your children eternal values, or are you focused on material, superficial appearances? Why is dress and appearance important in the worship service? Why is modesty important in the worship service? Who is to be the focus of the church service?

∾ What are "good works" a woman could adorn herself with? Would the general principle taught here apply to men also? How?

∾ Paul is writing that we may know how to conduct ourselves in the household of God, the church. How is a woman to conduct herself in a public worship service? Does Paul mention this idea in any other passage, or is this an isolated thought? Is Paul saying that women are not allowed to teach under any circumstance? Do we have biblical examples of women teaching? What is the specific context that Paul is addressing? If Paul gives a specific context, do we have the authority to take his instruction beyond that context? In other words, should I make more of this than Paul does? Are women ever allowed to teach in a church building? What about Sunday school? Vacation Bible school?

THOUGHT FOR THE WEEK

Last week we learned sound doctrine; we focused on knowing the truth. This week we have seen some ways we are to live out the truth in church. I realize the study this week has covered some very controversial areas. We must always conform to Scripture and never conform Scripture to our viewpoint.

Let me comment for a moment on 1 Timothy 2:15. It is a very difficult sentence to understand, and theologians disagree greatly over the meaning. Obviously, Paul does not mean women are saved in the spiritual sense through childbirth. What about women who have never had children? Can they never be saved? What about women who have children out of wedlock? Are they saved simply because they have had a child? You have already seen that the New Testament teaches salvation by faith alone. No one is absolutely sure of the meaning of the passage. Some think Paul is saying the woman who walks in godliness will be spared some of the pain involved in childbirth. Others believe the word *children* should be translated "child" and that this passage is a reference to the birth of the Christ child. All of us have been saved through the birth of the Christ child. Personally, I agree with Peter, who said some things Paul writes are hard to understand (2 Peter 3:14-16).

Now, concerning the issue of women teachers, does Paul forbid a woman to teach under any circumstance? Obviously not. Priscilla taught Apollos, and older women are to teach younger women. What is Paul's purpose in writing this letter? He is instructing us in how we are to conduct ourselves in church, the public worship service. The Greek words translated "to teach" and "exercise authority" are in the present tense—the present tense is also used in 1 Corinthians 14:34,35. The present tense shows that Paul is saying that a woman is not to continuously, as a matter of habit, teach or exercise authority over a man. The present tense does not forbid the act from ever occurring, but it is not to be the lifestyle, the norm. Paul seems to be saying that he would not allow a woman to be the teacher or to exercise authority in a public worship service. He is very specific, as you saw in 1 Corinthians 14. The position Paul takes is somewhat different than the two extremes we often see in church today. Knowing and living the truth is sometimes difficult, isn't it?

THE TRUTH ABOUT QUALIFICATIONS FOR LEADERSHIP

ᘎᘎᘎᘎ

DAY ONE

Only two weeks into this study and we have covered some serious topics. The benefits of knowing "thus says the Lord" surely make it worthwhile. Keep up the good work! God is pleased when His children study His Word.

This week we will study overseers and deacons, and like last week we will take one step at a time. Today read 1 Timothy 3. As you do, mark each reference to *overseer*[5] and *deacons*[6], including pronouns. You don't need to list what you learn yet. We'll do that tomorrow.

DAY TWO

To put yourself back into context, read 1 Timothy 3:1-7. When you finish, list in your notebook everything you learn about an overseer. Keep the list simple. If you find a word you do not understand, look it up in an English dictionary. Overseer, bishop, pastor, and elder all have the same qualifications. We sometimes use these words to make a distinction in position, but they are used interchangeably in the New Testament.

DAY THREE

Paul also lists the qualifications for an overseer in another passage. Today read Titus 1:5-9 and add any new insights to your list.

DAY FOUR

Were you aware that Paul was so specific in his qualifications for elders or overseers? He is just as particular when it comes to deacons. Read 1 Timothy 3:8-13. After you have read the passage (no shortcuts), list the qualifications for deacons in your notebook. As you did on Day Two, look up any words that are unfamiliar to you.

DAY FIVE

The only places where the office of a deacon is referred to in Scripture are Philippians 1:1 and the passage you have been studying. In the Greek, the word simply means "servant," but it may be translated several ways, such as "minister." Many people trace the origin of the office of deacon to Acts 6:1-6. Today I want you to look at three references that will help you understand how this word was used. The Greek word for *deacon* is used in these passages, but different English words are used to translate it. These will be quick and easy, so stay with me.

Read the following passages:

- John 2:5—the word *servants*
- Romans 13:3,4—the word *minister*

- Acts 6:1-6—The word for deacon is not used in this passage, nor are any of these men called deacons in any New Testament passage, but they do operate as servants.

DAY SIX

We have come to the third great doctrinal passage of this letter. You have looked at 3:14,15 several times to see why Paul wrote this letter to Timothy. Today we will look at this passage to learn about God the Father and Jesus the Son. Many people believe this passage is an early church hymn or possibly an early confession. It represents the faith of the early church. Read 1 Timothy 3:14-16. Read it slowly. After reading, mark every reference to *God* and every reference to *Christ,* such as *He.* Add to your list in your notebook what you learn about God the Father and God the Son.

When you finish, add the main idea of chapter 3 to your AT A GLANCE chart.

DAY SEVEN

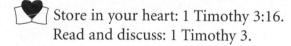 Store in your heart: 1 Timothy 3:16.
Read and discuss: 1 Timothy 3.

QUESTIONS FOR DISCUSSION OR INDIVIDUAL STUDY

Remember to support your answers from Scripture, not opinions.

- ๛ Discuss the qualifications for an overseer. What is the first qualification for an overseer? How do all the other qualifications relate to the first one? Are any of these qualifications moral issues? Which ones?

∾ What are the qualifications for a deacon? What does the word *deacon* mean? How is it used in the New Testament? What sort of things should deacons do? What should their job be in the body? How do these qualifications challenge your previous understanding of the role of deacons?

∾ What are the similarities between the qualifications for overseers and deacons? What are the differences? Must an overseer or deacon be married? Have children?

∾ Do you qualify to be an overseer? A deacon?

∾ If you are an overseer or a deacon, have you seen yourself as a servant of God? A servant of the body of Christ?

∾ What did you learn about Jesus Christ this week? From 1 Timothy 3:16, what did the early church believe about Jesus? What do you believe about Jesus?

∾ Discuss how 1 Timothy 3:16 reflects the heart of the gospel.

THOUGHT FOR THE WEEK

We focused our study this week on the qualifications of overseers and deacons. These qualifications represent sound discipline or proper behavior. The attitude and behavior of these men must be above reproach. God takes leadership within the body very seriously. He expects the best. How do you measure up? Sometimes people dismiss the need for these qualities in their own life by saying, "Well, I'm not a deacon" or "I'm not an overseer or a minister." But these qualifications look like qualities that should be present in the life of every believer. Ask God if there is a need for change in your own life.

In some circles, "husband of one wife" is the only qualification ever really considered. Literally translated in the Greek, this phrase is "one-woman man." The implication of this phrase has been widely discussed. Consider the following:

- One suggestion is that Paul means the husband of one woman at a time. This, in my opinion, is very unlikely. Polygamy was not practiced by the first-century Jews or Romans. It was never condoned in the church for any member, let alone a leader.

- It has also been suggested that Paul means the elders or deacons must have been married only once. If they were divorced or widowed, they could not be elders or deacons. This idea reads a lot into the text. Paul places no restrictions on widowers remarrying in any other passage. Later in this study we will see that young widows were commanded to remarry.

- Divorce is also presented as the restriction Paul is giving. Paul does not use the term *divorce*, although he was familiar with the word and could have said that very clearly. In my opinion, the qualification is much higher. The leader must be a man who is faithful physically, mentally, and emotionally to one woman: his wife. He must not be a womanizer in any sense of the word.

May we learn to use the entire list of qualifications when choosing our leaders, and not simply one. The well-being of the body of Christ is at stake.

THE TRUTH IS, GOD DOES CARE HOW I ACT

〜〜〜〜

DAY ONE

Only two more weeks to go. Can you believe it? We have covered some very serious ground. Are you ready for more? Let's go!

Your focus today is 1 Timothy 4:1-5, but to put yourself into context, read the entire chapter. When you finish, describe in your notebook those who "fall away from the faith" and the false doctrine they profess. Do this by asking yourself who, what, when, where, why, and how questions. For example, in 1 Timothy 4:1 you would ask, "To whom do they pay attention?" or "To what kind of doctrine do they pay attention?"

We have already seen sound doctrine and strange doctrine in chapter 1. Paul gives us more information in chapter 4. Review your notes from Week One and compare what you learned about strange doctrine in chapter 1 with what you learn in chapter 4.

DAY TWO

Paul has already made his views on marriage clear through his comments in 1 Timothy 2:15; 3:2,4,5,12; and as you will see later, 5:14. What about his views on abstaining from certain foods? Read 1 Timothy 4:1-10. Watch for the phrase *sound doctrine*[7] and mark it as you did in chapter 1. Watch for a contrast between what Timothy is to teach and what Timothy is to avoid.

DAY THREE

Up to this point we have seen very few instructions. During the remainder of our time together in 1 Timothy we will deal with a number of instructions. The result of sound doctrine is to be sound discipline or a proper lifestyle. We are to live out what we say we believe.

Today read 1 Timothy 4:6-16 and see how Timothy is to model sound doctrine before the congregation. You can do this by noting the instructions Paul gives Timothy. I mark instructions by placing an *I* in the margin next to the number of the verse. You may also want to list these in your notebook under INSTRUCTIONS.

There is a key repeated phrase in this passage: *these things*[8] (*them* in verse 15). Underline this phrase when you see it. *These things* refers to what?

Mark *teaching*[9] as you have done previously.

When you finish, record the main theme of chapter 4 on your AT A GLANCE chart.

DAY FOUR

Yesterday you saw some of the ways Timothy is to be an example of sound discipline to the congregation. Did you mark the instruction in verse 13? The church service was to include the public reading of Scripture. Scripture is powerful. It changes people's lives and brings them out of darkness into the light. Today I want to show you an example of the power of the Word, so you will understand the need to not neglect the public reading of Scripture. The book of Nehemiah describes a worship service that took place around 445 B.C. Read Nehemiah 8:1-12. Watch and see the power of the Word.

DAY FIVE

Today I want you to see how Timothy is to relate to specific groups of people. Read 1 Timothy 4:11–5:16. Watch the flow of thought. Since we want this Bible study to be practical and applicable to your daily walk, list in your notebook how Timothy is to respond to the four groups listed in 5:1,2. Are these instructions just for Timothy?

What about widows in the church? How are we to respond to them? One of the ways the world judges the church is by how we treat those in need. Orphanages and hospitals both originated from within the church. Paul gives very specific instructions on the care of widows. So you will be familiar with them, I want you to read 1 Timothy 5:1-16 and mark each reference to *widow(s)*, including pronouns.

DAY SIX

Today read 1 Timothy 5:1-16 again. After you have read the verses to put yourself into context, list in your notebook the qualifications of a widow who is to be taken care of by the church. Also list the characteristics of one who is not to be taken care of by the church.

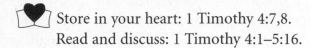

DAY SEVEN

Store in your heart: 1 Timothy 4:7,8.
Read and discuss: 1 Timothy 4:1–5:16.

QUESTIONS FOR DISCUSSION OR INDIVIDUAL STUDY

∾ What did you learn about those who "fall away from the faith"? To whom do they listen? What sort of things do they believe?

∾ Is there a connection between Paul's discussion of the law in chapter 1 and the false doctrine in chapter 4? What is it? What sort of restrictions do some churches place on people today that might be contrary to sound doctrine?

∾ Have you placed a high enough value on the Word that you will not twist or mishandle it? What does Paul spend his time describing: sound doctrine or unsound? Why? Where should our emphasis be? Do you know sound doctrine well enough to recognize the "doctrine of demons" if you hear it?

∾ Discuss Paul's instructions to Timothy. Do any of them apply to us today? How? What can you do to implement them in your walk? What kind of example are we to be? How exactly can you be that kind of example to your family? Your friends? Your coworkers?

∾ How are you to respond to older men? Younger men? Older women? Younger women? Discuss the underlying attitude Paul wants us, as believers, to have.

❧ Paul says we are to "honor widows who are widows indeed" (5:3). What is a "widow indeed"? How is this widow described? Who is to take care of widows? Who is the primary caregiver to be? What about the one who will not provide for his own family? Are you making preparation to provide for your parents? Grandparents? What is a "widow indeed" to be doing? Are there any age restrictions? What about younger widows? What is your church doing to identify and care for the widows in your congregation?

THOUGHT FOR THE WEEK

While there may not be a direct link between knowledge and behavior, there is a direct connection between belief and behavior. Let me explain. Everyone knows that smoking causes cancer and emphysema, but smokers keep on smoking and teens keep on starting to smoke. We all know the connection between sun exposure and skin cancer, but our beaches are filled with sunbathers working on their tan. Lack of knowledge? No. Lack of belief that they personally will be affected. Timothy was not a man who walked in knowledge only. He believed God. He believed the Word of God. His behavior reflected his belief. In 1 Timothy 4:6, Paul says that Timothy has been following sound doctrine, and he encourages him to continue to feed on the Word of God. In 4:7, Paul draws a direct contrast between the truth Timothy lives by and "worldly fables fit only for old women." Paul then tells Timothy to discipline himself for the purpose of godliness. In this context the discipline for godliness (i.e., proper Christian behavior) comes from being nourished on the words of the faith and on sound doctrine. The conduct Paul calls for in Timothy, and in you and me, is produced by a constant exposure to the Word of God. As I spend time in the Word of God, I begin to believe God and see the character of God. The result is a walk that honors God. How is your walk? Discipline yourself for godliness by being consistent in your study. In other words, we must know the truth and live the truth.

THE TRUTH ABOUT ELDERS AND MONEY

ᴥᴥᴥᴥ

DAY ONE

We have one week left in 1 Timothy. Did you have any idea there was so much in this short letter?

Paul has already described the qualifications for an elder. Today you will see some of the ways the church is to treat an elder. Read 1 Timothy 5:17-25. Mark the instructions in the text, and then list them in your notebook, just as you have been doing. The way we treat elders in the church is extremely important. I don't want you to miss these instructions.

You are through with chapter 5, so where will you record the main theme of this chapter? That's right.

DAY TWO

Read 1 Timothy 6:1,2, marking and then listing in your notebook the instructions you see. Also mark *doctrine*[10] as you've done before. Don't forget to add what you learn about doctrine to the list in your notebook. When you finish, cross-reference this passage with Colossians 3:22– 4:1. What kind of work ethic do you have? Are you doing your work as unto the Lord? Fortunately, God has delivered us from the evil of slavery in most countries of the world, but these principles would apply to our work relationships.

DAY THREE

Today I want you to read 6:3-10. As you do, mark the words *godliness*[11] and *doctrine*[12] or *sound words*.[13] Add what you learn about these words to the lists in your notebook. Watch carefully for the relationship between contentment, godliness, and money. You might want to go back and mark *godliness*[14] in 2:2,10; 3:16; 4:7,8, and add new insights to your list.

DAY FOUR

Read 1 Timothy 6:11-16. As you read, mark every reference to *Christ, God*, and *godliness.* Add to your notebook what you learn about each of these. Also mark the instructions and add them to your list.

Close your time today worshiping the King of kings by reflecting on what you have learned about Him during this study. The most awesome thing of all is that you have seen all of these things about Christ for yourself. It is so much more exciting to know what God has said than to know what someone has said about Him. It is the difference between firsthand knowledge and secondhand information.

DAY FIVE

We are nearing the end of our first five weeks together. This study has been rich in a knowledge of sound (and unsound) doctrine, godliness, and life instructions. Our prayer is that you will walk in a manner worthy of your calling.

Today we will spend our time in 1 Timothy 6:17-21. As you read, mark and then list the instructions in this passage.

One more time, turn to your AT A GLANCE chart and…that's right. You got it!

DAY SIX

As we close our study in 1 Timothy, I want you to take time to review what you have learned about doctrine and deeds, about knowing the truth and living the truth. Go over your list on true and false doctrines. Then review the instructions Paul gave to Timothy. True doctrine produces good deeds. Right beliefs produce right behavior. How do you measure up?

DAY SEVEN

Store in your heart: 1 Timothy 6:13,14.

Read and discuss: Colossians 3:22–4:1; 1 Timothy 5:17–6:21.

QUESTIONS FOR DISCUSSION OR INDIVIDUAL STUDY

∾ Discuss how the church is to treat an elder. What guidelines does Paul give for paying an elder? Does your church follow these guidelines? How are we to handle an accusation against an elder? What do we do if an accusation against an elder is true?

∾ What is our attitude to be at work? Toward those who have authority over us? According to Colossians 3:22–4:1, how are Christians to treat those who work for them?

∾ Discuss what you learned about godliness this week. What is the relationship between godliness and doctrine? What is the relationship between godliness, contentment, and money?

∾ Discuss what you learned about Christ this week. How will believing these truths affect your walk?

∾ Discuss all of the instructions you have seen this week. Do any of them apply to you? Why? Why not? Which ones?

∾ Timothy is to guard what has been entrusted to him. What has been entrusted to Timothy: good doctrine or bad? What is Timothy to avoid? What is the result of poor doctrine (6:21)? How is your doctrine? Do you know the Word of God well enough that you are able to guard what has been entrusted to you? If you don't, how do you know you haven't gone astray from the truth?

THOUGHT FOR THE WEEK

In chapter 6, verse 11, we are told to flee "these things." What things? I believe in the immediate context we are told to flee a wrong attitude toward those in authority over us (verses 1,2), flee false teaching (verses 3-5), and flee discontentment (verses 6-10). What are we to pursue? Righteousness, godliness, faith, love, perseverance, and gentleness. How? We have seen in this letter that right behavior is always produced by right beliefs. Deeds and doctrine are inseparable. We will know a tree by its fruit. Examine your life. What fruit are you bearing? Do you look like godliness, or like ungodliness? The apostle John said in 1 John 3:10, "By this the children of God and the children of the devil are obvious: anyone who does not practice righteousness is not of God, nor the one who does not love his brother." If your life doesn't reflect godliness and righ-teousness, then you might know about God, but you don't believe in Him. What are you fleeing from? What are you running toward?

You have studied the truth. Now live it.

Theme of 1 Timothy:

SEGMENT DIVISIONS

Author:

		CHAPTER THEMES
		1
		2
		3
		4
		5
		6

Historical Setting:

Purpose:

Key Words:

2 TIMOTHY

Introduction to 2 Timothy

꩜꩜꩜꩜

At first reading, 2 Timothy seems to be primarily about our responsibilities as faithful followers of Jesus Christ. This is true. We are taught that we must...

persevere even when it seems that everyone else is turning away,

protect the gospel from being twisted and watered down by false teachings,

pass on the good news to the faithful members of future generations, and

proclaim the truth, even in the midst of great opposition.

However, 2 Timothy shows us once again the marvelous truth that God is continuously working in our midst to provide what is needed as we obediently follow His instructions. He is a faithful God, worthy of our adoration and praise.

This book is about our responsibility to know His Word and to live it out daily.

INHERITING A FORTUNE

If a very wealthy and prominent individual wanted to bequeath his enormous estate to an individual who had superior attributes, exemplary characteristics, and an excellent reputation, would you qualify to be selected as the recipient of this great inheritance?

What attributes and characteristics should the beneficiary have? Let's see how the Bible describes such a man.

DAY ONE

This entire week will be dedicated to establishing the context of the book of 2 Timothy. These assignments will help you look at the book as a whole before you begin to look at each individual chapter. You will be led to discover the most obvious facts found in this brief letter. Facts about...

- the people—who are the people mentioned in this letter?

- the places—where are they?

- the events—what are they doing? What is happening during this time?

These facts will then lead you to see which subjects are repeatedly being discussed among or by these people. As the context is established, you can then more accurately interpret what the author is saying because you will know the "setting" in which he said it.

The "historical setting" refers to what was going on during the time the book was written. For example, were the people enslaved when the book was written? Were they in the midst of a conflict, a war? Was there a famine in the land? Was there tremendous persecution against them at that point in time? Were the people living in idolatry and immorality? etc. Once you determine the historical setting, you can then understand why the author said what he said, and what he meant by what he said.

If you haven't read the section in the front of this book entitled "How to Get Started," please stop and do so now. The instructions and information given in this section are essential to completing the following assignments throughout this study on 2 Timothy.

Are you ready? Here's your first assignment. To familiarize yourself with the content of the book and help you to see the book as a whole, read all four chapters in one sitting. It's a short book of only four chapters. Since 2 Timothy is a letter, it has an author and a recipient. Read it as though it is a letter you have just received from a friend. As you do, answer the following two questions—the answers will be very obvious. Record your answers on your AT A GLANCE chart found on page 106.

Who is the author?

To whom is he writing?

To complete today's assignment, answer the following questions and record your answers in your notebook under the title PAUL'S CIRCUMSTANCES. The answers will be found by reading 1:8–2:10 and 4:6-8. These answers will help you begin to establish the historical setting.

Where is Paul?

Why is he there?

How is he being treated?

When in his life is this occurring?

From what you've learned about Paul's circumstances, think about what was going on during these times to cause Paul to be where he was. Who put him there? Why did they put him there? What crime had he committed? On the AT A GLANCE chart on page 106, under the heading "Historical Setting," write a brief statement about what was going on during the time Paul was writing this letter.

DAY TWO

It is generally believed that Nero, the Roman emperor at that time, had set a large majority of the city of Rome on fire and had blamed the Christians. To divert the suspicion from himself, he ordered that the Christians be imprisoned and executed. Many Christians were put on poles alongside the highway and then, while still alive, set on fire to become human torches! Paul would not escape the psychotic madness of Nero. Here, in this prison, he would pen his last will and testament to Timothy, the beneficiary of all he possessed, the gospel ministry.

While some of the people mentioned in this letter were very supportive of Paul and his ministry, there were those who were not. In your notebook, make a chart similar to the one below and answer the questions for each of the passages. Remember, during this assignment focus *only* on the people who were *not* supportive of Paul.

Questions	1:15-18	2:15-18	3:1-9,13	4:3,4,10,14,15
Who are they?				
What did they do?				

Summarize what you've learned by adding these additional insights into what was going on during these times to the AT A GLANCE chart under "Historical Setting" on page 106.

DAY THREE

Read all four chapters of 2 Timothy again. Then mark each mention of the recipient's name or a pronoun that refers to him, as you did in 1 Timothy.

Prepare a place in your notebook to make a list of all you learn about Timothy. (About one sheet of 8½" x 11" paper, front and back, should be enough.) Put the title TIMOTHY in the center of the page at the top. On the left-hand side of the page, put the subtitle "2 Timothy." List all the facts you learn, including the chapter and verse number, under that subtitle. For those of you who have not done this before, the illustration on the next page will help you understand what you need to do.

TIMOTHY

2 Timothy

1. Timothy was Paul's beloved son (1:2).
2. Timothy had a sincere faith (1:5).
3. Timothy _____ (chapter, verse), etc.

Look carefully at each mention of Timothy that you marked, and write down any truths about him that you have gleaned from the passage. Remember, you may not learn something significant at every marking of his name, so don't feel pressured to write something for each marking. (Sometimes the recipient's name is mentioned by the author when he reveals something about himself, such as in 1:3: "I constantly remember you in my prayers." Here you learn that "Paul prays for Timothy." The emphasis is on what you learn about Paul, not on what you learn about Timothy.)

Don't forget to ask the who, what, where, when, why, and how kinds of questions at each marking.

Also, this is very important: As you make your list on Timothy, *do not* include those statements in which Paul tells Timothy something specific to do. Those are instructions. (Most of the time when Paul instructs, the *you* is understood and not printed in the text, such as in 1:8. Therefore, your attention may not even be drawn to an instructive statement, and it may not even be a consideration for your list because there is no marking in that verse. However, sometimes the *you* is printed [4:5], and this may cause you to think you need to mark the pronoun and then put something on the list. Look at each marking carefully.) Put only those things on your list that help you learn something specific about Timothy the person. We will look at the instructions later in this study.

DAY FOUR

Today, you're going to learn some more about the recipient, Timothy. Your assignment will take you to the books of Acts, 1 Corinthians, and Philippians.

Read Acts 16:1-5 and, as you do, mark each mention of the recipient the same way you did in 2 Timothy. Add what you learn to your Timothy list in your notebook under the new subtitle "Acts 16:1-5."

Do the same for 1 Corinthians 4:17 and Philippians 2:19-24.

DAY FIVE

Read 2 Timothy again. This time as you are reading, answer the question, "Why did Paul write Timothy this letter?" In other words, what was Paul's purpose in writing to Timothy? Before deciding upon your final answer, review what you learned about Paul, his circumstances, the historical setting, and what you learned about Timothy. Summarize your answer as briefly as possible and record it under the title "Purpose" on the AT A GLANCE chart on page 106.

DAY SIX

Turn to the AT A GLANCE chart on page 106 and find the list of key words. You will be dealing with all of the key words as you complete this study. However, today we will deal with just one of them: *gospel*. Read through the entire book and mark every reference to *gospel* and its synonyms in a distinctive manner. (I mark *gospel* and its synonyms with a purple cloud like this gospel. You don't have to use the same color and symbol that I've suggested, but it does need to be different than the colors and symbols you've already used. This makes it easy to distinguish between the words, and to see which words are mentioned the most.)

Read 2 Timothy again, making a list of what you learn about the gospel in your notebook. Be careful to write down what the verse says about the gospel, not your interpretation of what it says. For example, the first mention of *gospel* is in 1:8.* Your list may look like this:

GOSPEL

Do not be ashamed of *the testimony of the Lord* or of me His prisoner (1:8).

Join with me in suffering for *the gospel* according to the power of God (1:8).

DAY SEVEN

Store in your heart: 2 Timothy 1:14.

Read and discuss: 2 Timothy; Acts 16:1-5; 1 Corinthians 4:17; Philippians 2:19-24.

QUESTIONS FOR DISCUSSION OR INDIVIDUAL STUDY

∽ Who wrote this letter?

∽ Who is the recipient of this letter?

∽ Where is Paul? How does he describe the way he is being treated?

∽ Why is he there? What crime had he committed?

∽ When in his life did this occur?

---

*See notes 1–9 under 2 Timothy, pp. 131, 132 for the NIV, KJV, and NKJV equivalents for the key words in chapter 1.

∾ Who was not being supportive of Paul during these days? What did they do?

∾ What did you learn about the historical setting during these times?

∾ What did you learn about Timothy in 2 Timothy? Acts 16:1-5? 1 Corinthians 4:17? Philippians 2:19-24?

∾ What attributes did Paul ascribe to Timothy?

∾ Of these attributes, which ones describe you? Which ones do not describe you? What could you change in your life to make the missing attributes become an accurate description of you?

∾ How would you describe the relationship between Paul and Timothy?

∾ Why did Paul write this book?

∾ Why did he choose to write to Timothy?

∾ What did you learn about the gospel?

THOUGHT FOR THE WEEK

Someone once said that sufferings and persecutions are the schoolhouse that teaches us who we really are. It is in the difficult times that our responses to adversity reveal our true character. We can sometimes "fake" our reactions to unfavorable situations, but true, genuine, overwhelming difficulties and tragedies can reveal much about us. Our response to an unexpected death…a sudden, overwhelming financial need…an unusual, unanticipated reaction from a coworker, friend, or family member…a devastating situation, can sometimes bring to the surface some emotions, thoughts, and words we never thought were in us.

Sometimes the thermometer of response can truly reveal the temperature of our heart.

This week you saw for yourself the contrast between the faithful few and the misguided many. The responsibility of passing on the gospel treasure is still there regardless of our response to persecution. Paul passed the gospel ministry to Timothy in the midst of the most difficult times, when the penalty of faithfulness was death. He knew Timothy's character. Timothy had proven himself to be faithful over and over again.

And then there were those who had chosen, by an act of their own will, not to remain faithful and carry out their responsibilities, but rather to abandon the Word and work of God.

What makes the difference? Could it be that in those times of great difficulty, knowing the Word of God has something to do with the ability to go through difficult times and respond appropriately? Paul knew the Word of God. Timothy could teach the Word of God the same as Paul. Then there were those who turned away from it, distorted it, and opposed it. What can build character in a man? What can develop those inherent attributes that lie dormant within us all? Could it be the knowing of His Word?

Well, bless you for completing this week's assignments and for continuing to dig into His Word. You have proven that you can "be diligent to present yourself approved to God as a workman who does not need to be ashamed, handling accurately the word of truth" (2 Timothy 2:15). Continue, my friend, to be diligent.

TO HEAVEN OR TO HELL?
THAT'S THE QUESTION

"What happened to my mama when she died?" she asked.

"Well…that depends," he answered.

Reminiscing, she softly spoke, "She was a good person…though she didn't go to church…and I never saw her read the Bible…She used to tell me all the time that she was praying about this or that…She was real tenderhearted… why, she would give you the shirt off her back if you needed it."

Silence filled the air, and then in desperation she asked, "She's in heaven, isn't she?"

What would be your answer to that question? Would you know what the Bible says? If you want to know the long-term benefits of being a believer, complete this week's homework. Then you'll be able to give a biblical answer if you're ever faced with a similar scenario.

DAY ONE

For the next four weeks, you will study 2 Timothy one chapter at a time. Last week you learned about Paul's circumstances. Today, read chapter 1 and mark every reference to *Paul*, including the pronouns. (I usually mark the name of the author of a letter with a blue ballpoint pen. I simply draw a circle around his name, like this: ⟨ **Paul** ⟩ .)

Now make a list in your notebook entitled "Paul" and record the new insights you learn about him from this chapter. (Leave some space for what you will learn about him in the remaining chapters. Also, don't forget to note the chapter and verse of each truth.) Be sure to ask the 5 W's and an H questions such as, "What does Paul say about himself?" "How does Paul describe himself?" etc.

Now review your list on Paul and look for any comparisons that he makes regarding himself. What does the comparison Paul makes about himself in verse 3 and the comparison he makes about Timothy in verse 5 have to do with their gospel heritage? How does this relate to the purpose of the book? (Remember, last week you discovered "why" Paul was writing to Timothy.)

DAY TWO

You're right—you're going to read chapter 1 again today. This time you're going to mark the key words in this chapter. Last week you saw that the key word *gospel,* or one of its synonyms, appears in all four chapters of this book. However, there are some key words that only appear in a specific chapter or chapters.

As you read through chapter 1, make sure that you marked *gospel* and all of the synonyms you find listed on the next page. If you are just starting to study the Bible using the inductive method, you may have missed some of these synonyms. That's all right. It's understandable.

You will have instructions to help you develop this skill as you go through these New Inductive Study Series Bible study courses. If you did miss any of the synonyms, mark them now and add what you learn from the text to the list in your notebook.

> *gospel* (verses 8,10)
>
> *testimony of our Lord*[1] (verse 8)
>
> *for which*[2] (verse 11)
>
> *For this reason*[3] (verse 12)
>
> *the standard of sound words*[4] (verse 13)
>
> *treasure*[5] (verse 14)

Now read the chapter once for each of the following key words, marking each word and its synonyms in its own distinctive manner, and making a separate list in your notebook of what you learn about each. Leave some room in your notebook. These will appear later in other chapters.

> *remember (recall, mindful, remind)*[6]
>
> *suffering (suffer, chains)*[7]
>
> *ashamed (turned away)*[8]

DAY THREE

In Paul's letters you will often find that he instructs, exhorts, warns, and charges. This is true in this letter. He charges Timothy in 4:1: "I solemnly charge you in the presence of God and of Christ Jesus...." He warns Timothy in 3:1: "But realize this, that in the last days difficult times will come." Read chapter 1 again today and look for any instructions that Paul gives to Timothy. An instruction is a specific "do this" or "don't do that" command. Mark these instructions in the text in a distinctive way. (I put a capital *I* in the margin next to the verse where the instruction begins. Then I underline the instruction with a straight line using a black ballpoint pen. This helps me "spot" the instructions easily.) Make a list of these in your notebook under the title INSTRUCTIONS. Don't forget to leave plenty of space to add the other instructions you will find in the following chapters. Again, use words directly from the text. For example, the first instruction given in chapter 1 is found in verse 8: "Do not be ashamed of the testimony of our Lord or of me His prisoner."

DAY FOUR

There are no warnings or charges in this first chapter. However, there are instructions and exhortations. An exhortation is a statement that Paul makes for the purpose of encouraging Timothy, to propel him to some future action or behavior. For example, Paul calls Timothy his "beloved son" (verse 2). In this statement, Paul not only reminds Timothy of their intimate relationship, but also encourages or exhorts him to act like his beloved son in the future, in spite of these most difficult circumstances.

Read chapter 1 again today and look for the exhortations. You may want to mark them with a capital *E* in the margin also, and put a squiggly line like this: ~~~~~~ under the exhortation in the text. Make a list of EXHORTATIONS in your notebook, using words from the text as much as possible. Leave space in your notebook for additions to the list from the remaining chapters.

DAY FIVE

Read chapter 1 again and mark in a distinctive way every reference to *God*, including any pronouns *(who, His,*

He, Him) and synonyms (*Lord,* when used to refer to God). As was stated in 1 Timothy, sometimes it may not be clear from the context if the word refers to God or to Jesus. In those cases, mark it as *God* and as *Jesus* both, and include the truths learned on both lists. Once you've completed marking all the references, make a list of what you learn in your notebook.

Now go back through your list and review what God provides. For example, "1:2—God gives grace, mercy, and peace." If you have time, you could make a separate list in your notebook of GOD'S PROVISIONS. If you do, don't forget to leave enough room to record what you learn about God's provisions in the other chapters.

DAY SIX

When you did your list on God yesterday, did you notice that Paul introduced a new subject in verses 9 and 10? Look at these verses and review them again. What is he talking about? What's the subject?

Read these verses slowly, asking the 5 W's and an H questions after each phrase. As you read these verses, record what you learn about salvation. Make a separate list for what you learn about JESUS, THE SAVIOR.

Determine the main theme of chapter 1 and record your summary statement of what it's all about on the AT A GLANCE chart on page 106.

DAY SEVEN

 Store in your heart: 2 Timothy 1:9,10.
Read and discuss: 2 Timothy 1.

QUESTIONS FOR DISCUSSION OR INDIVIDUAL STUDY

∾ How does Paul describe himself? What does he say about himself?

∾ Whom did Paul compare himself with in 1:3? Whom did Paul compare Timothy with in 1:5? What do these two comparisons have to do with the purpose of the book? In other words, how did the use of these comparisons help Paul accomplish his purpose?

∾ What contrast did Paul make between himself and "all in Asia" in chapter 1?

∾ What comparison did Paul make between himself and Onesiphorus?

∾ What did you learn about the gospel? Where in chapter 1 is the gospel defined? What two things did Jesus do when He appeared that are a part of the "good news"?

∾ What caused Paul's suffering and imprisonment?

∾ Who was ashamed of the gospel and of Paul? Who was not ashamed? Are you ashamed of the gospel or of those who preach it in inappropriate settings?

∾ What instructions did Paul give to Timothy? Were all the instructions about the gospel? Why would Paul be instructing Timothy about the gospel?

∾ Why would Paul instruct Timothy not to be ashamed of the testimony of the Lord or of him? According to what you learned about Timothy last week, was Timothy being ashamed like those in Asia?

∾ Why would Paul instruct Timothy to join with him in suffering for the gospel?

∽ What standard of sound words did Paul want Timothy to retain? Where in chapter 1 is that standard found?

∽ What treasure did Paul want Timothy to guard? According to chapter 1, from what would Timothy have to guard the treasure?

∽ What exhortations did Paul give to Timothy? Which came first: an exhortation or an instruction? When you deal with people, what do you do first: exhort or instruct?

∽ What did you learn about God? What does God give the believer? What does He not give the believer?

∽ According to verse 9, how were Paul and Timothy saved? How were they not saved?

∽ How were Paul and Timothy called? What kind of calling was it?

∽ To whom was salvation granted? What does granted mean in light of the context of these two verses?

∽ In whom was salvation granted? When was salvation granted in Christ Jesus? When was salvation revealed to man? When did Christ appear as Savior? What did Christ do when He appeared as Savior?

∽ What was Paul facing at this particular moment in his life? Was it important for him to know that Christ had abolished death and brought life to light? Was it important for Timothy to be reminded of this truth at this time in history?

∽ How did Timothy hear about this salvation?

∽ How is a person saved? Is it by his works? On what verses of Scripture do you base your answer?

THOUGHT FOR THE WEEK

Relationships are the canvas upon which our very lives are painted. Everything we do, think, and say seems to come from our multicolored relationships. We act like our forefathers. We are biased in our opinions because of the culture that raised us. We are recognized geographically by our speech. We are a portrait of our past associations.

Paul begins this last letter by revealing his intimate relationship with his close friend Timothy...his "beloved son." He closes chapter 1 by sharing about another close, personal friend, Onesiphorus.

He then moves quickly, by the stroke of the pen, to remind us of the importance of a godly heritage from family relationships by mentioning his forefathers and Timothy's foremothers.

He also shares in the last verses of chapter 1 that painful experience that came when "all who are in Asia turned away from me." Among them were two men, Phygelus and Hermogenes, whom he called by name—revealing something more than just a casual relationship.

And nestled in the midst of these relationships of friends and family, Paul very profoundly draws our attention to that most important relationship: the one we have with God, our heavenly Father.

Good friends. Bad friends. Faithful. Unfaithful. Godly family. Ungodly family. When physical death comes to pay a personal visit, life boils down to one very critical, important relationship: the relationship we have with God the Father. Everything else is temporary. In the end, the only relationship that determines a person's eternal destiny is the personal relationship he or she has or doesn't have with God the Father through the Savior, Christ Jesus. No one earns salvation by works (the good things they do or the bad things they don't do). Salvation was given to us in Christ Jesus from all eternity, according to God's purpose and grace. Jesus is the one who abolished death and brought life and immortality to light when He appeared on this earth to die on a cross as our substitution in payment for our sins. We can live forever. We can have eternal life. We can know our eternal destiny is heaven, not hell. No wonder Paul could live his last days in the light of the glorious gospel while facing certain death. He knew that, for him, death had been abolished! Eternal spiritual separation from God had been done away with. He knew he would spend eternity in heaven. You, too, can know. Do you know where you will spend eternity? What will happen to you when you die? Heaven? Hell? Have you trusted in Jesus Christ as your personal Savior?

CAN A REAL CHILD OF GOD BE RECOGNIZED?

ᴖᴖᴖᴖ

We've all seen people who profess to be Christians but act like the devil. How can you tell who the true Christians are? How can you identify those who are false? Are there any characteristics to look for? Let's see what Paul has to say to Timothy about this.

In this last will and testament, we find Paul reminding his beloved son whom he should entrust with the gospel treasure and whom he should avoid. He not only told Timothy how he could tell the difference, but also how he should respond to both groups of people.

Can you tell the difference? How do you respond to those who oppose you? How are you supposed to respond? Let's see what the Bible says.

DAY ONE

This week you will spend all your time in chapter 2. We will go through the chapter verse by verse, rather than reading through the chapter a number of times looking for various key words and truths. In verse 7 of this chapter, Paul instructed Timothy, "Consider what I say, for the Lord will give you understanding in everything." You will find that to be a helpful prayer this week as you study this chapter. There are several passages in this chapter that are going to require more than just a casual look if you are going to gain the maximum benefit. As you study this week, continually ask God to help you understand what Paul is saying, why he said it, and how that statement relates to the verses around it. Now let's begin digging into this gold mine of spiritual truths that promise to clarify some confusing issues about those who name the name of Christ.

In your previous two weeks of studying 2 Timothy, your assignments have instructed you to mark certain key words and characters and to make lists of the truths you've been learning about them. Also, you've been asked to make a list of the instructions and exhortations. You'll need to have all those lists by your side as you work through chapter 2 in order to add new truths to these lists.

Also, if you haven't made a key word bookmark with your distinctive colored symbols for each, you may want to do that now. It will not only save you a lot of time as you go through these remaining chapters, but it will also serve as a reminder in completing this week's assignments. (Making a bookmark is also explained in the "How to Get Started" section, pages 7–14, in the front of the book.)

For your convenience, the things you have been instructed to mark so far are listed below.

Key Words

gospel (testimony of the Lord, for which, for this reason, the standard of sound words, treasure)

remember (recall, mindful, remind)

suffering (suffer hardship,[9] chains) (In chapter 2, mark *imprisoned*[10] and *imprisonment*.[11])

ashamed (turned away) (Add *gone astray*[12] to this list for chapter 2.)

Key Characters

Paul

Timothy

The other people

God (also a list on "God's Provisions")

Jesus

Instructions

Exhortations

This week as you come to each day's assignment, you will be asked to look at a certain portion of chapter 2. This may be one verse or several verses at a time. You will not be instructed each time to mark the key words (*gospel, remember*, etc., and their synonyms), the key characters (*Paul, Timothy*, etc., and their pronouns), the instructions and exhortations, and to add the truths you learn from marking these to the corresponding lists. I'll just instruct you to mark anything on your bookmark and add what you learn to the appropriate list. This way I won't have to say the same details over and over again each day. You'll know what I mean. Just look at your bookmark; mark any key word, character, instruction, or exhortation that appears in those verses; and add the truths to your ongoing lists. Remember, you may add new key words to your bookmark at any time along the way if they come to the surface in one of these remaining chapters.

All right, I think with those general instructions out of the way, you're ready to begin.

Now, even though you will be looking at chapter 2 verse by verse, take a few minutes to read through chapter 2 to get an overview of this chapter—the "big picture." As you read this chapter, keep asking yourself the following 5 W's and an H kinds of questions:

What is this chapter about?

How do the verses and paragraphs relate to each other?

Why did he say what he said when he said it?

Now read verses 1 and 2 again. Mark anything on your bookmark and add what you learn to the appropriate lists. By the way, there are several new synonyms for *gospel* that appear in chapter 2 that were not in chapter 1. Since *gospel* is such an important key word in 2 Timothy, I don't want you to miss these. The new synonyms to mark are the following:

the things which you have heard from me[13] (2:2)

these[14] (2:2)

word of God[15] (2:9)

word of truth (2:15)

these things (2:14) or *the truth* (18,25)

Add these to your bookmark. The *gospel* synonyms *for which*[16] and *for this reason,*[17] which you marked in chapter 1, also appear in this chapter. Be sure that you don't overlook them. Also, if you missed marking any of these synonyms in the Week One assignment, mark them now and add new insights to the list in your notebook. Don't be discouraged if you didn't see these as synonyms the first time you marked the key word *gospel*. As you continue to practice this inductive method of study, it will become easier to spot the synonyms.

Read verses 1 and 2 and reason with them by asking the 5 W's and an H questions. If you will practice asking these kinds of questions, you will be amazed at how much you will learn. *The way you'll know which question to ask is by reading the text first to see what kind of question the text demands.* For example, if you read the verse and it mentions a person, you may want to ask a "who" type of question such as, "Who is talking?" or "To whom or about whom is he speaking?" or "Who is mentioned in this verse?" If you read the name of a place, the questions could be, "Where is this event happening?" or "Where is he going?"

Let me further illustrate how you could ask these kinds of questions by giving a few questions that might be used in reasoning through these first two verses, and then I'll let you develop the questions for the remaining verses.

- What instructions does Paul give Timothy in these verses?

- Where is Timothy to find the strength? (Maybe this answer should also go on the "God's Provisions" list that you started last week in your chapter 1 assignments.)

- What "things" did Timothy hear from Paul? Where in chapter 1 did you also see that Timothy heard some things from Paul? (This will help you see how

Scripture interprets Scripture, as well as how chapter 1 relates to chapter 2.)

• Why did Paul say that Timothy was to entrust these things to "faithful men"? What kind of men did Paul talk about in chapter 1:15-18? Also, in contrast, what kind of man was Onesiphorus?

• What did Paul expect the faithful men to do with the teaching Timothy would give them?

• What does this concept in verse 2 have to do with the purpose of the book?

I hope this helps you get started in the reasoning process. It is going to be very important that you continue this process throughout the remaining verses of this chapter. If you don't, then the verses will seem to be unrelated and the chapter will seem to be fragmented. That's not the way it is. They are related, and Paul is making a point. You will want to discover that point.

In your notebook, make a two-column chart like the one below. Leave yourself plenty of room to record what you learn from the chapters that follow.

CHARACTERISTICS OF BELIEVERS/UNBELIEVERS	
Characteristics of Believers	Characteristics of Unbelievers

Look back over 2:1,2 and note any characteristics you would attribute to believers.

DAY TWO

Today read 2:3-10, marking any key words from your bookmark and adding what you learn to the appropriate lists.

Now read verses 3-6 again. When you finish, make a chart in your notebook like the following and fill it in. The information for the chart will be found by reasoning through these Scriptures by asking the 5 W's and an H questions.

PAUL'S EXAMPLES			
What is the example Paul uses?	How does Paul describe the example? (if any)	What does the example do or not do?	Why does the example do it or not do it?

Now look at the information you recorded in the PAUL'S EXAMPLES chart and think about what kind of person Paul is describing in these verses. Believer? Unbeliever? Record any attributes on your CHARACTERISTICS OF BELIEVERS/UNBELIEVERS chart in the appropriate column.

DAY THREE

Read 2 Timothy 2:11-13. Scholars differ as to where this "trustworthy statement" may have originated. To help you better understand this entire statement, in your notebook rewrite these verses into four individual statements, each starting with *if*.

The way in which the word *if* is used in all four of these statements means that it is an accepted fact, rather than being hypothetical or suppositional. In other words, it is a true statement that can be relied upon. It is indeed trustworthy. For example, you could restate the first statement this way, "It is an accepted and reliable fact that since we died with Him, we shall also live with Him."

Now review what you learned about the gospel from verses 7-10. How does each one of the "if" statements relate to these truths about the gospel? (Pay particular attention to verse 10.)

Also, add any new attributes you glean from verses 11-13 to your CHARACTERISTICS OF BELIEVERS/UNBELIEVERS chart.

DAY FOUR

Read 2 Timothy 2:14-21, marking as needed from your bookmark and adding what you learn to the appropriate lists.

Add the new attributes you glean from these verses to the CHARACTERISTICS OF BELIEVERS/UNBELIEVERS chart in your notebook.

DAY FIVE

Read 2 Timothy 2:22-26, marking from your bookmark and adding what you learn to the appropriate lists.

Again, add the new attributes you glean from these verses to the CHARACTERISTICS OF BELIEVERS/UNBELIEVERS chart.

DAY SIX

Start today by going back to chapter 1 and reading through those verses, again recording any attributes you glean out of these verses on your CHARACTERISTICS OF BELIEVERS/UNBELIEVERS chart.

For the remaining time today, your assignment is going to be reflective in nature. It's one of those assignments you could read and respond by saying, "I don't need to do that" or "I've already done that." I hope you won't be tempted to skip over this opportunity, but will allow God, through the Holy Spirit, to really settle this issue of how to distinguish between those who belong to Him and those who don't. Here's the assignment. Read through the CHARACTERISTICS OF BELIEVERS/UNBELIEVERS chart and think about each of the qualities listed under "Characteristics of Believers." Ask yourself this question: "Do I have these attributes in my life?" If not, "How can these attributes be manifested in my life?"

Now prayerfully read and think about the characteristics of unbelievers. Ask yourself, "Do I have any of these attributes in my life?" Using this chart as a guide, how would you describe yourself thus far: believer or unbeliever?

If your conclusion is "unbeliever," go back and review your list under GOSPEL and your list under SALVATION. You can change by believing on the Lord Jesus Christ. You don't have to stay the same.

If your conclusion at this point in the study is that you are a believer, how are you responding to those who oppose you? With gentleness? Are you wrangling about words? Are you quarreling over foolish and ignorant speculations?

Summarize the main theme of chapter 2 and record that statement on the AT A GLANCE chart.

DAY SEVEN

 Store in your heart: 2 Timothy 2:15.
Read and discuss: 2 Timothy 1:15-18; 2:1-26.

QUESTIONS FOR DISCUSSION OR INDIVIDUAL STUDY

∾ What instructions are in chapter 2?

∾ What exhortations are in chapter 2?

∾ What did you learn about the gospel in chapter 2?

∾ What "things" did Timothy hear from Paul? Where in chapter 1 did you also see that Timothy heard some things from Paul?

∾ Why did Paul say that Timothy was to entrust these things to "faithful men"? What kind of men did Paul talk about in 1:15-18? Also, in contrast, what kind of man was Onesiphorus?

∾ What did Paul expect the faithful men to do with the teaching Timothy would give them?

∾ What does this concept in verse 2 have to do with the purpose of the book?

∾ What three examples did Paul give in chapter 2? How did he describe them? What did each of the examples do or not do? Why did the example do it or not do it?

∾ To what does the "trustworthy statement" in verses 11-13 relate?

∽ How does the "trustworthy statement" relate to the three examples? According to the context, what does Paul refer to when he talks about the "large house" in verse 20—the one with the "firm foundation of God"? From what must a man cleanse himself in order to be "prepared for every good work"?

∽ What are the characteristics of an unbeliever?

∽ What are the ways we are to respond to unbelievers?

∽ What are the characteristics of a believer?

THOUGHT FOR THE WEEK

In our study of chapter 1 last week, we learned that we are not saved according to our works but according to His purpose and grace (1:9). However, this week in our study of chapter 2, we learned that we are known by what we do: our deeds, our actions, our reactions. One example given to us was the example of the good soldier who does not entangle himself in the affairs of everyday life. This leads us to conclude that the bad soldier does. He is known to be a good or bad soldier by simply observing the habitual pattern of his lifestyle. Does he continually, consistently entangle himself in the affairs of everyday life or not?

Also, in the illustration regarding the large house, there were vessels to honor and vessels to dishonor—the good vessels and the bad vessels. Here Paul is talking about the visible church—those local congregations that exist with a firm foundation of those who are His, and who abstain from wickedness. However, when people come together to hear the Word of God preached, there are both believers and unbelievers present in the audience. Some of the unbelievers could be searching for a relationship with the God of this universe. They earnestly desire to have a relationship with God and are being drawn to Him, but they haven't yet discovered how to enter into that relationship with Him through the Savior, Christ Jesus. Other unbelievers may have different motives in mind. Regardless, the ones who set themselves apart and abstain from wickedness (abstain from doing and participating in wicked activities) are the ones who will be useful to the Master and prepared for every good work, showing through their actions that they are the good vessels.

Our actions do bear witness of the condition of our heart. Titus 1:16 states it clearly, "They profess to know God, but by their deeds they deny Him, being detestable and disobedient and worthless for any good deed."

We are not saved by our works, but we are recognized by them. Our works prove whose we are. If you ever have a question about someone, watch him and see what he does, how he reacts, how he relates to other people. Listen to what he says and how he says it. Don't look at just one incident. Look for the habitual, continual pattern of his life. What he does will speak clearly.

*A*RE *W*E *L*IVING IN THE *L*AST *D*AYS?

Immorality has crept into every profession, every financial stratum, every community, almost every age, every sacred institution. It seems that no one is exempt. Nothing is off-limits.

Murder, theft, drug addiction, alcoholism, rape, gang war, meaningless shootings in schools and homes and businesses, racism, divorce, and abortion are at an all-time high.

Are these the last days? How do we know if we are living in the last days? We're not the only ones who have asked this question—so have other people who have gone before us. How did they know what to look for? What did they do? What can we do?

What is the answer to this moral decline? Is there an answer? Where can we turn? To whom can we turn? More specifically, what can you and I do to make a change? Can one person like me or like you make a difference?

There is *one thing* that can make a difference. If you will incorporate this *one thing* into your daily life, you can have an impact on your family, your friends, your coworkers, your community, your nation, and the world. What is this *one thing*? Come, let us now reason the Scriptures together!

DAY ONE

Read chapter 3 to get the flow of thought of this chapter.

In your notebook, quickly review what you learned about the historical setting of this book, the attributes of Timothy, and the purpose for the book. Also, briefly review your CHARACTERISTICS OF BELIEVERS/UNBELIEVERS chart. This should put you back in the proper context for your study this week. (Remember that when 2 Timothy was written, it was one continuous letter without the chapter and verse divisions. That's why it's important to keep reviewing the entire flow of thought and not separate one chapter from another.)

Mark as needed from your bookmark and add what you learn to the appropriate lists. (When marking your key words, mark *sufferings, persecutions,*[18] and *persecuted*[19] the same way that you marked *suffering* earlier.) Synonyms to mark for *gospel* are *the truth, my teaching,*[20] *the things,*[21] *sacred writings,*[22] and *Scripture.* Make sure that you mark the three instructions in this chapter (verses 1,5,14), as well as any exhortations.

Keep in mind that the phrase "the last days" is commonly understood to mean those days beginning with Jesus' ascension to heaven and ending with His return. It is not understood to mean a short, specific period of time just before His return. In other words, we are living in "the last days" now.

DAY TWO

Today read 2 Timothy 3:1-5. As you do, add the descriptions given of these men in the last days to the CHARACTERISTICS OF BELIEVERS/UNBELIEVERS chart.

By the way, the actual Greek word used in the original manuscripts for *men* (verse 2) is more generic than just a description of a masculine person. The word used literally means "people" or "mankind," which would include both men and women. You could read verse 2, "For *people* will be lovers of self."

Some of the characteristics are familiar terms and need no further explanation. However, there are a few of these terms that may not be crystal-clear to you. The term *lovers of self* is pretty clear—it means what it says. However, the term *revilers* is not commonly used in the popular English language of today. So as you add each of these terms to your chart, look at the following list to see if a further explanation of that specific characteristic is given in this brief glossary of terms. The brief definitions are designed to enhance your understanding of exactly who these people are so that you may recognize them quickly and make sure that none of these characteristics are in your life.

> *disobedient to parents*—a person who resists the authority of his parents, leading him to resist all other authority, both human and divine
>
> *revilers*—a person who uses his speech to cause harm to people, attempting to "tear them down" in his conversations with other individuals
>
> *irreconcilable*—a person who will not accept a truce but continues in his enmity and unforgiveness
>
> *malicious gossips*—a person who intentionally thinks up evil reports and accusations and falsely accuses someone else. (This word is the same word used to describe the devil.)

without self-control—a person who is void of any self-imposed restraints over his passions and lusts. (Note that in 2 Timothy 1:7, God has given believers power, love, and discipline. The word *discipline* could be translated "self-control.")

brutal—a person who is untamed, savage, and wild in his actions and attitudes

treacherous—a person who betrays any confidence and trust placed in him—a traitor

conceited—a person who knows it all and cannot be told anything by anybody

lovers of pleasure rather than lovers of God—a person who loves what is pleasurable to himself rather than what pleases God; a person who is controlled by satisfying his passions—food, drink, recreation, entertainment, success, sex, etc.— rather than being controlled by what pleases God

holding to a form of godliness—a person who holds to an appearance of religion, a mask of godliness. This person would attend church as a ritual and embrace some of the traditions of religious activity (like celebrating Christmas and Easter), but would not have a personal relationship with Christ.

DAY THREE

Read verses 6 through 9 today. What do these people do in the last days? Add these things to the CHARACTERISTICS OF BELIEVERS/UNBELIEVERS chart. Also, make a list in your notebook of what you learn about these WEAK WOMEN.

Read Romans 1:18-32 and notice the similarity of these lists describing unbelievers.

DAY FOUR

Start today by reading verses 10-11 and adding the characteristics attributed to Timothy to your CHARACTERISTICS OF BELIEVERS/UNBELIEVERS chart. In this instance you will have to draw out of the text the characteristics of believers from what Paul said about Timothy. For example, Paul said, "But you followed my teaching, conduct," etc. Timothy was a believer. Believers will "follow the teachings of Christ," "conduct themselves in a way to reflect that they are followers of Christ," etc.

To get a better understanding of the persecutions Paul endured at Antioch, Iconium, and Lystra, read 2 Corinthians 11:24-27.

Add what God did for Paul in response to the many persecutions (verse 11) to your GOD'S PROVISIONS list in your notebook.

Now read verses 12-13 and record what you learn about believers and unbelievers on your CHARACTERISTICS OF BELIEVERS/UNBELIEVERS chart.

Also make sure you recorded the exhortations found in verses 10-13.

DAY FIVE

You're close to the end of chapter 3! In these last two days we'll be looking at one of the most important passages of Scripture. Stay with us; we're almost done.

Read verses 14 and 15 and, in order to help you reason through the Scriptures, answer the following questions:

- What was Timothy to do?

- What was he to continue in?

- What things had he learned and become convinced of?

- Who do you think taught him those things?

- What were other people doing during these days, according to what you previously learned about the historical setting?

- When was Timothy first exposed to the "sacred writings"?

- Who do you think may have shared those sacred writings with him when he was a child?

- What were the "sacred writings" able to give him?

- What did the wisdom do?

- The wisdom that leads to salvation is in the Bible, but we must appropriate it through what?

- Our faith to save us is in whom?

If you've learned anything additional regarding the subject of salvation, you may want to add these new insights to the SALVATION list in your notebook. (You made this list in Week Two, Day Six.)

DAY SIX

The final day of this week's personal study time is an important one. You will want to look at these last two verses carefully and thoroughly.

First of all, read verses 16-17. The word *all* in the Greek language is the word *pas*. Some translate this word "every." Believe it or not, the very definition of this one word has spurred much debate among theologians. Some theologians interpret this verse to mean that each individual Scripture might not be inspired, but together the whole is inspired. Other theologians interpret it to mean *all* or *every* Scripture is inspired by God, with the understanding that this implies "each and every Scripture making up all Scriptures" are inspired by God. (We embrace the latter interpretation that each and every Scripture making up all Scriptures is inspired by God. Also, we need to note here that because of the context of 2 Timothy, Paul is talking about only the Old Testament Scriptures in this particular passage. Paul does include the inspiration of New Testament Scriptures in 1 Corinthians 2:9-16.)

Read 1 Corinthians 2:9-16.

"Inspired by God" simply means that Scripture is God-breathed.

Make a list below of the four things that Scripture is profitable for as you see them in 2 Timothy 3:16:

1. _____

2. _____

3. _____

4. _____

Look at the following definitions for each of these four terms. Then write in your notebook your new understanding of this verse in your own words.

teaching—The Word of God teaches us with absolute authority what is right.

reproof—The Word of God convicts us when we think, say, or do something wrong.

correction—The Word of God shows us how to correct what we've done wrong and to make it right.

training in righteousness—The Word of God trains us in righteousness, showing us how to do it right the first time.

Now look at verse 17. Again, the word *man*, used in the term "man of God," is the same word that was used in 3:2. It should be understood as "the man or woman of God, the people of God."

The word *adequate* means, "exactly fitted." The word *equipped* means "completely qualified so you can accomplish your destined purpose."

Now write in your notebook your new understanding of verse 17.

Also, don't forget to record your summary statement for chapter 3 on the AT A GLANCE chart.

DAY SEVEN

Store in your heart: 2 Timothy 3:14.

Read and discuss: Romans 1:18-32; 2 Corinthians 11:24-27; 2 Timothy 3.

QUESTIONS FOR DISCUSSION OR INDIVIDUAL STUDY

∾ How were the people in the last days described? Were they believers or unbelievers? How does this compare with what you learned in chapter 2?

༶ What did the men do?

༶ How were the weak women described?

༶ What did Paul instruct Timothy to do regarding these men?

༶ Will these men of the last days go unnoticed in what they are doing?

༶ What was the end result of those people who rejected God in Romans 1:18-32?

༶ How did Paul describe Timothy in this chapter?

༶ What persecutions did Paul go through that were described in 2 Corinthians 11:24-27? How did Paul go through those persecutions and sufferings? How will we go through persecutions and sufferings? How does this relate to what we learned about how we suffer in 1:8b?

༶ What can you expect if you desire to live godly in Christ Jesus? How does this line up with the teaching that once you're saved you won't suffer anymore, that God desires you to always be healthy, wealthy, and happy?

༶ What exhortations does Paul give Timothy in this chapter?

༶ What was Timothy to continue in? What things had he learned and become convinced of? Who do you think taught him those things?

༶ What were other people doing during these days, according to what you previously learned about the historical setting?

∾ When was Timothy first exposed to the "sacred writings"? Who do you think may have shared those sacred writings with him when he was a child?

∾ What were the "sacred writings" able to give him? What did the wisdom do? Wisdom that leads to salvation is in the Bible, but we must appropriate it through what? In whom is our faith for salvation?

∾ For what is Scripture profitable?

∾ How would you explain the meaning of verses 16 and 17?

∾ Are verses 16 and 17 talking about the entire Bible—the Old Testament and the New Testament? If not, why not?

∾ Where in the Bible is the inspiration of the New Testament discussed?

∾ What role does the Word of God play in salvation? What role does the Word of God play in the life of believers?

∾ What is the one thing that Timothy had incorporated into his life even from early childhood that made the difference between him and the men of the last days? What will make a difference in your life?

∾ Are you continuing in the things you are learning from His Word? Are you convinced that they are true? Are you following the teachings of Christ? Can someone tell you are a believer just by watching your conduct?

∾ Are you adequate, equipped for every good work? Which comes first: the Word of God or the work of God? Which comes first in your life?

∾ Are we living in the last days? What can you do to make a difference?

Thought for the Week

A recent survey showed that 80 percent of the people who went to a local church, heard the gospel preached, and made a commitment to Him, quit going to church within just a few months because they said they saw no difference in the lives of the "Christians" and those who did not profess Christianity.

We now have megachurches that offer everything from arts and crafts classes to recreational facilities; everything from the Mom's Day Out nursery programs to senior adults extended care; everything from summer camps for teenagers to marriage retreats for couples; and everything from single-again activities to college mission trips. But immorality is infiltrating almost every family.

We feed the hungry, we clothe the naked, we evangelize sinners, we assist the devastated, we encourage the downtrodden, and we give millions of dollars to the unfortunate. But no matter what we do, our world is crumbling around us.

We are liberated as we sing in our services with absolute freedom, we are entertained by humorous sermons, we are enlightened by pulpit discussions on relevant issues, and we even feel better every day of the week because we attended an hour service once a week. Yet we are bound by feelings of guilt, burdened by the past, and stymied by fear of the future.

One would think that, with all we're doing, we would have more of an impact on the world around us. Are we doing some good? Yes, I think so. But what's wrong? Why aren't we seeing more improvement in the moral condition of our world? What is the answer? Could it be that we are placing such an emphasis on programs that minister to the physical, emotional, mental, financial, vocational, and recreational pleasures of people that we've abandoned ministering to their greatest need—the spiritual—where we could help them to learn what pleases God?

Maybe we've gotten the horse before the cart. Maybe we need to return to the biblical pattern. Could it be that we are so busy performing all this work in the name of God through these many programs that we've not had the time to study His Word? It is the Word that makes us adequate, equipped for every good work.

Are we living in the last days? I think so. Today most people are holding to a form of godliness but are lacking the power thereof. Everyone is doing what is right in his own eyes, without regard to what the Word of God has to say about the issues. What can you do personally to make a difference? What did Paul do? What did Timothy do? Do that! Study His Word (2:15). Entrust His Word to faithful men so they can teach others also (2:2). Live out what you are taught (3:10). Continue in the things you have learned and are convinced of (3:14).

WHAT WILL THEY SAY ABOUT YOU WHEN YOU'RE GONE?

Just by studying His Word through this course, you are making a difference!

If it were left up to your mate, your children, and your grandchildren, what would they want engraved on your tombstone?

If it were left up to your parents, your brothers, and your sisters, what would they engrave?

Your friends? Your neighbors? Your boss? Your co-workers? Your business acquaintances? Your pastor, priest, or bishop? What would they engrave?

DAY ONE

Read chapter 4 just to get the flow of thought. Now read through chapter 4 again, this time marking every reference to *Jesus*. Add these new insights to your list. (Remember that when the word *Lord* is used, if you cannot distinguish who it is, either God or Jesus, just mark it both ways and add the truths to both of your lists.) You'll learn some awesome truths about Jesus in this chapter. Don't miss them.

Jesus is described as Lord (1:2), as Savior (1:10), and as Master (2:21). How is He described in chapter 4?

Review your list on Jesus, putting a check mark (✓) beside each truth that shows you something that Jesus does. For example, in 1:2, you learned that Jesus "gives grace, mercy, and peace." As you read these truths, put your name into the truth as you read it. For example, read 1:2 this way: "He gives me grace, mercy, and peace." Whatever He would do for Paul, He will do for you! Think about this especially in chapter 4.

DAY TWO

Today read through chapter 4 again, marking all the instructions and exhortations found in the chapter. Add these to your ongoing lists.

Notice the instructions in verses 9 and 21. Does it sound as though he's saying the same thing twice? Can you sense the heart of Paul reaching out to his beloved son in these final hours? Relate this to what Paul said about Timothy in 1:4.

DAY THREE

As you read through chapter 4 today, mark in the same manner as before every reference to the following:

Paul (I, my, me)

synonyms for gospel—the word, sound doctrine, the truth, teaching,[23] and proclamation[24]

synonyms for suffering—hardship[25]

Add what you learn to your lists. When you finish your lists, think about all that Paul has gone through—the beatings, the sufferings, the persecutions, the imprisonments, the abandonment by people who were close to him, the opposition to his teaching, the twisting of what he taught to make it heresy—and yet, note the attitude he has about the future. Wow!

Our joy should not be in our present circumstances or what has happened to us in the past. Our joy should come from what we are anticipating to happen to us in the future!

DAY FOUR

Today we want to look more closely at the "charge" Paul gives to Timothy. Read 2 Timothy 4:1-5 and answer the following questions. As you answer these questions, give some thought to each one so that you may grasp the heart of Paul in these closing moments.

- In whose presence is Paul charging Timothy?

- Why do you think Paul would give this strong instruction in these circumstances?

- What is Paul solemnly charging Timothy to do? (Look closely and slowly at these verses so that you can see that first Paul tells Timothy *what to do,* and then he tells him *when* and *how* he is to do it. Just ask the 5 W's and an H questions of the text, and you will see the answer clearly.)

- What is Paul charging Timothy to do? When is Timothy to do it? How is Timothy to do it? Why is it so important that Timothy accept this charge? What is hanging in the balance? (As you answer this question, remember the historical setting you've established, and especially what you learned last week in your study of 2 Timothy 3:1-9 and 13.)

DAY FIVE

Now read 2 Timothy 4:3,4 again, and mark the pronoun *they* in a distinctive way. Does this seem to be a continuation of the description he was giving in chapter 3 of the men in the last days? Add what you learn about them to the CHARACTERISTICS OF BELIEVERS/UNBELIEVERS chart in your notebook.

DAY SIX

To finish our study on believers/unbelievers, read 2 Timothy 4:6-18. Add any insights you glean from the people mentioned in these verses to your CHARACTERISTICS OF BELIEVERS/UNBELIEVERS chart. Pay particular attention to the way Paul describes himself in verses 6-8.

Today your assignment is one of reflection. Review your CHARACTERISTICS OF BELIEVERS/UNBELIEVERS chart. As you do, think seriously about each characteristic that you've placed on your chart. As a pattern of life, not just on occasion, which characteristics best describe you and your lifestyle?

Record a brief summary statement about the main theme or main subject of 2 Timothy 4 on the 2 TIMOTHY AT A GLANCE chart. Now that you have completed your overview study of 2 Timothy, you will want to summarize the main theme of the entire book and record it on the chart.

Also fill in all the blank spaces on the chart that you possibly can. Once you've finished, take a moment or two and review all the insights you have recorded on this chart. These are your own observations! Now you have a better understanding of the book of 2 Timothy than you did before.

Obviously, there are some things you saw in 2 Timothy that you probably wished you had had more time to study, but at least you now have a good overview of this "last will and testament" from the great apostle Paul to his beloved son, Timothy. (We have a more in-depth Bible study on the book of 2 Timothy. Of course, the deeper you go, the more time it requires. Should you be interested in learning more about this course, contact us at 800-763-8280, visit our website at www.precept.org, or fill out and mail the response card at the back of this book.) Also, now would be the time to transfer your pertinent notes from this study into your Bible, although maybe not every marking and maybe not every list.

DAY SEVEN

 Store in your heart: 2 Timothy 4:5.
Read and discuss: 2 Timothy 1:8; 2:3,15; 3:11,12; 4.

QUESTIONS FOR DISCUSSION OR INDIVIDUAL STUDY

∾ What did you learn about Jesus from chapter 4? How does Paul describe Him in chapter 4? How does Paul describe Jesus in other parts of 2 Timothy? What does Paul say that Jesus does? What will Jesus do for you?

∾ What instructions did Paul give to Timothy in chapter 4? What exhortations? Are the instructions found in verses 9 and 21 similar? How do they compare with the instruction found in 1:4? What do you sense about the heart of Paul as he writes these types of statements?

∾ What did you learn about *gospel* this week? What are we to do regarding suffering? How does this truth about suffering relate to what you learned in 1:8; 2:3; and 3:11,12?

∾ What does Paul "solemnly charge" Timothy to do? In whose presence? Have you ever felt that God had abandoned you and was nowhere around as you went through some difficult times in your life? Are these feelings correct? When was Timothy to carry out this charge? How was he to do it? Why was it so important for him to accept this charge in light of the days in which he was living? How does this apply to us?

∾ Can you "preach the Word" if you don't know the Word? What instruction does Paul give Timothy in 2:15?

∾ What did you learn about *they*? What will "they" do and not do? Is this a continuation of his description of believers/unbelievers? Are we living in "the last days"?

∾ What did Paul say about himself in this chapter that would be exemplary behavior that you should follow?

∾ Which set of characteristics best describes you: believer or unbeliever?

THOUGHT FOR THE WEEK

God has given us all that we need to do all that He created us to accomplish while here on planet Earth. He has given us grace, mercy, and peace. He has given us power to suffer, love for our enemies, and self-control for those times when it seems we're going to be overwhelmed and not in control of our own emotions. He has given us confidence that He is able to keep safely that which we have entrusted to Him. He gives us strength in our times of weakness and understanding in all things. He is not restricted by our limitations, is not moved from faithfulness by our failures, and is not unaware that we belong to Him. He delivers, equips, judges, punishes, and rewards. He compensates our enemies according to their deeds, stands by us when no one else will, and uses us to speak when no one wants to hear. He will deliver us from every evil deed, bring us safely to His heavenly kingdom, and when this life is over, He will welcome us into our permanent, eternal dwelling place to live with Him forever!

God has given us His Word and instructed us not to be ashamed of it but to suffer for it, to retain its standard, to guard it from all manner of evil, to entrust it to faithful men, to handle it accurately in our studies, to continue in it every day of our lives, and to preach it when it's convenient and when it's not. His Word gives us wisdom that leads to salvation and is profitable for teaching, reproof, correction, and training in righteousness so that we might be adequate, equipped for every good work.

Paul knew this. Paul shared this with us. No wonder Paul could stand at the end of his life and declare with certainty: "I have fought the good fight, I have finished the course, and I have kept the faith." What do you know about Him and what He's given you? What will you say at the end of your life?

Theme of 2 Timothy:

SEGMENT DIVISIONS

Author:

Recipient:

Historical Setting:

Purpose:

Key Words:

gospel
word
suffer
(hardships;
persecutions)
endure(d)
faith
ashamed

GOD'S PROVISION	PAUL'S EXAMPLE	CHAPTER THEMES
		1
		2
DELIVERED OUT OF PERSECUTION	ENDURED PERSECUTIONS	3
		4

TITUS

INTRODUCTION TO TITUS

How surprised you are going to be when you get into this short but powerful and practical letter! If you've been troubled by some people who profess Christ and yet live and believe very differently than you, Titus will be an eye-opener. And if you have wondered if there is any hope for our mixed-up, confused, hurting society, you'll find the answer here. You'll see it for yourself, and then you'll be convinced and know how to order your own life so that you won't dishonor the Word of God.

Just think of what would happen if you would study this course with a group of people who want to take their Christianity seriously! It would be awesome because there would be more of you to live out the truths you are about to discover, and together you would have a far greater impact.

So if you are not doing this in a group study, ask God whom you are to ask to join you—either in person, over the telephone, in a couple's study, or over the Internet. Then watch what God does in just three short weeks.

WHAT ARE THE REQUIREMENTS FOR A GODLY LEADER?

It is always good to take time to reflect on the important issues of life—to measure them by the plumb line of God's Word and make sure that you are living according to the precepts of God, rather than according to the traditions of man. For instance, have you ever examined why you attend the church that you do? Why do you put yourself under the leadership and authority of those who oversee your church? What are the leaders of your church like? On what basis are they selected for leadership? How do their lives impact yours and influence the direction of the church?

Are there men in your church who are upsetting church families through their actions, speech, and beliefs? If so, is the church dealing with them? Or isn't this the responsibility of the church?

What a week is in store for you as you discover for yourself what the book of Titus has to say about the character, lifestyle, and responsibilities of the elders or overseers of your church.

DAY ONE

Because Titus is such a short book—short but so rich, so practical, and so needful—take your 15 minutes of study time to simply read through it. This will help you familiarize yourself with the book as a whole. When you come to any geographical locations, double underline them with a green pen. When you finish, record in your notebook who wrote the book and to whom it was written.

DAY TWO

Today we're going to begin to dig a little deeper and see what we can learn about the writer of this short letter and the man to whom it was written. Read chapters 1 and 2. Use one color to mark every reference to the author and another color to mark every reference to Titus, its recipient. Make sure that you mark any pronouns.

When you finish, make two columns in your notebook—one for the author, the other for the recipient. Then list what you learn from marking each reference. Use the 5 W's and an H—who, what, when, where, why, and how—to help you think through this list.

DAY THREE

Read Titus 3 today, once again marking the references to Paul and Titus. When you finish, list in your notebook any new insights you learn about either of them.

Now then, faithful one, look at your list. What do you see that gives you the historical or geographical context of this letter or insight into Paul's reason for writing? Or to put it in 5 W's and an H terms, see if you can discern *why* it was written. *What* was Paul's purpose? Record this on the AT A GLANCE chart on page 129.

You discover the historical setting of a letter or book by discovering any references to what was occurring at the time, looking at the circumstances of the author or recipients, and noting any references to geographical locations.

Record all this in your notes under the general title The SETTING AND PURPOSE OF PAUL'S LETTER TO TITUS.

DAY FOUR

Today we want to delve deeper into chapter 1. One of Paul's reasons for writing to Titus is stated in verse 5. Read verses 5-9 carefully and then list in your notebook what you learn about elders and/or overseers. Title your list "Godly Elders." (This is review for you if you did the 1 Timothy study, but review is good.)

As you saw in 1 Timothy 3:1-7, Paul gave Timothy a list of qualifications for bishops or overseers. Many people believe that an overseer or bishop is the same as an elder. Go back and review your list from 1 Timothy. Then compare the two lists.

When you finish, think about those in your church who hold positions similar to these. Do they hold to the same criteria as those in Titus?

DAY FIVE

Now, did you notice in your reading of Titus 1 the contrast between the two types of men? In Titus 1:5-9, Paul lays out the qualifications of elders. Then in verses 10-16 he mentions another group of men who, he says, must be silenced and reproved.

In your notebook, list what you learn about these men. Before you make your list, you may want to mark every reference to them in a distinctive color or way to be sure that you don't miss something.

Now read through chapter 1 again and mark every occurrence of the word *deed(s)*.[1] You will mark these throughout the book.

When you finish, compare the two lists you made these past two days. What have you learned? How do these biblical insights translate into today—your times, the church in which you worship? Think about it, and if you are a man, ask yourself which list describes you.

DAY SIX

Read through Titus 1 again and mark every reference to *God*. It's exciting to see what you learn from listing what the text says about God! Taking the time to do this simple exercise will help you build a sound understanding of who God is. It's the basis of biblical theology.

Now wrap up this week's study by putting your theme on the AT A GLANCE chart on page 129.

DAY SEVEN

Store in your heart: Titus 1:1,2 or Titus 1:16—a good reminder that not everyone who professes to know God really does!

Read and discuss: Chapter 1, especially verses 5-16.

QUESTIONS FOR DISCUSSION OR INDIVIDUAL STUDY

∞ From your cursory reading of the book of Titus, what did you discern as Paul's reason for writing? What verses led you to this conclusion?

∾ What did you learn about Paul, about Titus, and about their relationship?

∾ What was Paul's first instruction to Titus in this epistle? What prompted this?

∾ What did you learn about elders? Discuss the list you made, the qualifications of such leaders, and their responsibilities.

∾ How does your church determine who is going to hold positions of responsibility like these? What have you learned that you can apply to your own life?

∾ Does such a description help you in selecting the church you should attend? In what way?

∾ What did you learn about those men defined in Titus 1:10? Describe their character and their deeds or lifestyle.

∾ What is the church's responsibility with respect to this group of people? Why?

∾ What did you learn about God from studying Titus 1?

∾ In what special way has God spoken to you this week? Is there something you have learned or been convicted about?

THOUGHT FOR THE WEEK

If everything rises and falls on leadership, then how essential it is that we, as those chosen of God, make sure that we know what God says we need to do to set in order our homes, our lives, our priorities, our values—and to appoint godly leadership over the church.

To do so we need a knowledge of the truth which is according to godliness. If we don't have this knowledge and are not being led by godly elders and overseers in the church, then we can be certain that men who profess to know God but deny Him by their deeds will step in to fill the void.

This is why the appointment of godly elders, overseers, pastors, deacons—whatever title your church or denomination gives them—is so critical. Now that you have seen these truths with your own eyes, how are you going to pray for your church and support it in these matters?

Truth for the sake of knowledge alone will not accomplish the work of God. We must live out the Word of God and put it into practice. If we don't, could we possibly be categorized as those who profess to know Him but by our deeds deny Him?

Think upon these things. Ponder them in your heart. Hold fast the faithful word which is in accordance with the teaching you have seen this week. You will never regret it, for you will bring God such pleasure, and isn't that why we were created?

WHAT DOES GODLINESS LOOK LIKE IN ME?

ᘛᘛᘛᘛᘛ

There are so many voices in our world today telling us how to behave, what to believe, urging us to look out for "number one." How can you listen and watch without getting confused and being led astray? There is only one way, and that is by having a knowledge of the truth which is according to godliness. If you want truth on how to live, you'll see it this week as you abide in Titus 2.

DAY ONE

Your assignment today is a simple one. Read Titus chapters 1 and 2, watching the flow of thought. Remember that this was a letter from Paul to Titus and contained no chapter or verse divisions. Chapters and verses were added later for the sake of helping us identify where something is found.

As you read chapter 2, watch for the different categories of people mentioned in this chapter. List them in your notebook. Then as we progress, we'll see what Paul has to say about each group, including Titus, his true child in the faith.

Also, since you began marking the word *deed(s)*[2] in 1:16, continue marking it in chapter 2.

DAY TWO

Read chapters 1 and 2 again. This time mark every reference to the following:

1. *The word of God* and any synonyms used for *the Word.*

2. Any reference to *sound doctrine* or *doctrine.*[3] The Greek word for *doctrine* is *didachê*, which is translated "doctrine," "teaching," or "instruction." The word for *sound* is *hugiaino* and means "healthy, whole."

When you finish, think about what you have seen just from marking these two words and their synonyms. Write in your notebook what you think Paul's concern is when it comes to the Word of God and sound teaching or doctrine. Also note your insights into why Paul was so concerned.

DAY THREE

To begin, read Titus 2 again and make sure that you have marked every reference to Titus. (Remember, you were to have marked references to Titus during your first week of study. Record this list in your notebook.)

How do Paul's specific instructions to Titus in 2:1,15 relate to the rest of the content of this chapter? Write your insights in your notebook under chapter 2.

Now read Titus 2:2-5. List what Paul says the older men are to be like. When you finish the list, make sure that you understand what each word in the list means. *Temperate* means "to be sober, controlled." The Greek word for *sensible* (self-controlled or temperate), *sophron,* means "of sound understanding, disciplined."

If you are an older man, how do you measure up? Are there any areas that you need to work on? If so, put a star beside them, and then turn it all into a matter of prayer.

Next, list what the older women are to do. As you make this list, separate it from what the younger women are to be taught and, therefore, are to do. Make a separate list for the younger women. "Workers at home" is the translation of the Greek word *oikourgos,* which means "keeper of a house."

DAY FOUR

Truth dispels lies, and God's Word is truth. Therefore, since so many men and women have become confused as to the role and responsibility of women, you will find it enlightening to review 1 Timothy 5:3-16 and think about what you learn about women.

In this passage Paul gives instructions to Timothy with respect to widows—older widows and younger widows. As you have seen, although he is speaking with respect to widows, there is much to be gleaned in reference to women in general in regard to their character, behavior, and responsibilities.

Go back and review the INSTRUCTIONS list you made in Week Four, Day Three of the 1 Timothy study. How does this list compare to Paul's instructions to the older women in Titus 2:3-5?

Note: When you come to 1 Timothy 5:14, the Greek word for "keep house" is *oikodespoteo,* which means "to be a master of the house" or "to govern or manage a home or the domestic affairs of a family."

Man or woman, husband or wife, have you believed a lie or been led astray in your thinking as to what God says about women—their character, behavior, relationships, and responsibilities?

If God has spoken to you in a specific way, record it in your notebook.

DAY FIVE

Now let's return to Titus 2:6-14 where Paul turns to the young men. Watch the connecting word he uses: *likewise.* Likewise what? Mark the words *sensible*[4] or *sensibly*[5] and any synonyms that refer to them. Go back and mark *sensible*[6] in Titus 1:8. When you finish, think about what you have learned and record it in your notebook.

Is this a word that characterizes our generation, or is it even encouraged in our times? What do you think would be the end result of such a quality?

List Paul's instructions regarding young men, then measure the behavior of the young men who are in your family. What is being instilled in them?

Finally, list the instructions for bondslaves. Although you might not live in a society that has slaves, do you think this could be compared to those who serve under other people? If so, what is to be learned? Think about it, and record it in your notebook.

DAY SIX

This last day of study this week is going to be so rich as we focus on Titus 2:11-15. In verse 11 you read that "the grace of God has appeared."

What has this grace of God done? List your insights from Titus 2:11-14 in your notebook, and then examine yourself in the light of them.

Mark each reference to *Jesus Christ*. Then list what you learn about Jesus from these verses. This is where worship comes from: looking at someone's worth and giving him the glory due him. You might want to spend some time in worship when you finish.

As you look at Titus 2:15 and the words *these things*, compare it with *speak the things* in 2:1. Record in your notebook what you observed "these things" to be.

If you have time, review what you have written in your notebook this week. Think about all you have seen and how God would have you live in the light of it. Remember, the goal of inductive study is transformation: "the knowledge of the truth which is according to godliness" (Titus 1:1). Truth embraced is more than intellectual assent. It changes us from being ungodly in our conduct to being more like God. When we embrace truth, rather than simply acknowledging it, it will produce good deeds.

Record your theme for chapter 2 on page 129 on the AT A GLANCE chart.

DAY SEVEN

Store in your heart: Titus 2:11,12 (or, if you have time, through verse 14).

Read and discuss: Titus 2.

Questions for Discussion or Individual Study

∾ What are the things Paul instructs Titus to speak? Simply give a general summarization since you will discuss these things in detail later.

∾ Discuss what the older men are to be and how this compares with the elders.

∾ What did you learn this week with respect to women? What is to be the focus of their lives? Discuss what you observed in Titus and Timothy. How does this compare with the way women are living today?

∾ What did you learn about young men? Include Paul's instructions to Titus and, as you do, explain from the text why it is acceptable to include Titus.

∾ Could Paul's instructions regarding bondslaves be applied to those who work for other people? Discuss this, and if you think it applies today, note how it would be lived out in a very practical way.

∾ What does the appearance of the grace of God do? Discuss how all this is lived out in a practical way.

∾ What did you learn about Jesus Christ from this chapter? How does it relate to all that is written in these 15 verses?

∾ What did you learn from marking *the word of God* or *doctrine* in chapters 1 and 2 and its relationship to our lives? Discuss how the lives of those in the church today measure up to what the text teaches us.

∾ In Titus 2:15, Paul instructs Titus to speak these things, exhort, and reprove with all authority. The verbs *speak*, *exhort*, and *reprove* are all present imperative verbs. In other words, Titus is commanded to do this habitually, continually. Why? What would happen if this were done in churches today?

THOUGHT FOR THE WEEK

What are the things fitting for sound doctrine that Paul wanted Titus to speak? They are truths about our character, our behavior, our relationships, our roles—good deeds which adorn the doctrine, the teaching of God.

Because our theology has become so "me-centered," so focused on signs, wonders, healings, and spiritual experiences, we have forgotten that God has a standard for His people.

- It is a standard of holiness that instructs us to deny ungodliness and worldly desires and to live sensibly, righteously, and godly in this present age. How often do you hear this on television—the media that can spread every wind of doctrine across the country with the speed of sound and light?

- It is a standard that, if adhered to, would correct many of our social problems and restore us to our proper roles as men and women. It would keep society from self-destructing, which it is doing at an alarming rate in North America and around the world.

To live with such a standard is not impossible. Jesus Christ has redeemed us from every lawless deed and purified us for Himself. And what does this purification bring? It produces within us a zeal, a passion for good deeds. If you do not have this zeal and passion, then you should examine your relationship with God, for something is terribly out of order.

May we be pioneers again in the cause of holiness! May our passion be not to dishonor the Word of God, but to adorn it in every respect. And may we pray for each other and for the church accordingly, holding forth the Word of life without compromise or hypocrisy in the midst of this crooked and perverse generation. May they see by the very way we choose to live that our God is worthy of honor, power, glory, and dominion forever and ever because we honor Him as God.

WHAT MAKES YOU DIFFERENT?

Do you remember what you were before you met Jesus Christ—before you were born again, regenerated, and given the Holy Spirit? Would remembering this help you be more considerate of other people who are where you have been? If so, this is going to be a profitable week for you and for the world you touch—your world that is watching you and trying to figure out why you believe as you do and why your life is different from theirs!

DAY ONE

Read the last and very valuable chapter of Titus. As you do, mark each reference to *deed(s)*[7] as you've done previously. Then list everything that Titus teaches with respect to deeds. It will be an invaluable list.

DAY TWO

Paul's letter to Titus, his child in the faith, is filled with instructions—things he wants his "son" to do. As he brings his brief letter to a close, the instructions come in almost a staccato sequence in chapter 3. Much of what Paul says will also pertain to us as "children in the faith."

Read the first two chapters of Titus. Every time you come to an instruction—a command given by Paul to Titus—mark it to indicate that it is a command.

Then summarize and list each command in your notebook under PAUL'S INSTRUCTIONS TO TITUS. Note I said "summarize"—in other words, record the essence of each command, and number each one so that it is easier to see.

When you finish, it would be good to spend some time in reflection. If Paul were writing these things to you as a child of God, how would you measure up?

DAY THREE

Today read Titus 3:1-3. In your notebook, add to the list the instructions given in these verses. When you finish, look up the following cross-references and note them next to the command they pertain to, along with any notes you might want to have for future reference:

> Romans 13:1-7
> 2 Timothy 2:24,25
> 1 Peter 2:12

Finally, with what in the list does Titus 3:1 connect? What lesson do you learn from it? Record this in your notebook. You'll add more to this list on Day Six, so leave room in your notebook.

DAY FOUR

Read Titus 3:3-8 aloud. These are awesome verses, so rich in truth. Note the contrast between verses 3 and 4.

Mark every reference to *God* in a distinctive way. Also mark in distinctive ways each reference to *Jesus Christ* and to the *Holy Spirit*,[8] including pronouns. When you finish, list what you learn about each from marking the references.

If you have time, go back and review the references that you marked on *God* in chapter 1. Add any new insights to your list if you did not do a list earlier.

DAY FIVE

Read Titus 3:4-8 again. Observe your markings, and review what you listed about God, Jesus Christ, and the Holy Spirit. Now take a fresh look at these verses, and list everything you learn from them about salvation. As you do this, notice the relationship of "good deeds" to salvation, if you didn't already see it when you made your list on deeds.

Finally, stop and meditate on what you have learned about God and salvation in these last two days, for this is a "trustworthy statement," and God wants you to speak confidently about these things.

Examine yourself. Are there good deeds that show you are a child of God, or by your deeds do you deny Him? If you are not a child of God, ask Him to save you from your sin and bring you into His family. If you are a child of God, take time to rejoice in all that He has done on your behalf.

If you have asked God to save you and have asked Jesus to become your Lord and Savior, record the date in your Bible so that you will remember on what day to celebrate your spiritual birthday. Also, let us know because we have a "welcome to the family" gift for you.

DAY SIX

This is your final day of study. How we commend you for your diligence! Our hearts so rejoice over your hunger and thirst for righteousness and your desire to know God and His Word.

Read Titus 3:8-15 and mark every instruction. Finish the list in your notebook. When you're done, compare 3:10,11 with 1:9,13; 2:15.

Now go forward to engage in good deeds (really, occupations) so that you can contribute to the work of God by meeting pressing needs. When you live, work, and give accordingly, your life will not be unfruitful.

What is the main theme of chapter 3? Record it on the AT A GLANCE chart.

DAY SEVEN

 Store in your heart: Titus 3:1,2 or 3:5-7.
Read and discuss: Titus 3.

QUESTIONS FOR DISCUSSION OR INDIVIDUAL STUDY

∾ What did you learn from Titus 3:4-8 with respect to salvation? Discuss your insights and what such understanding can mean to you practically.

∾ What did you learn about the work of God, Jesus Christ, and the Holy Spirit from the book of Titus?

∾ When you made your list on deeds, what did you observe about the deeds of a person? What do our deeds demonstrate and validate or invalidate? Where do good deeds fit with respect to salvation? Discuss what you believe to be good deeds.

∼ What are Paul's instructions to Titus in this third chapter? Discuss each one, noting whether or not it is applicable to our lives and, if so, how.

∼ Why are we to show every consideration for all men? On what basis?

∼ From Titus 3:3, what do you learn about the work of salvation in a person's life?

∼ What is the most significant thing you have learned personally from the book of Titus? Why was it the most significant?

∼ How important do you think the message of Titus is for the church today? What do you think you can do to help people understand the precepts laid out for us in Titus?

∼ Has God spoken to your heart in a personal way so as to redirect your path in any way at all? If you're studying Titus in a group, share with the group how God has spoken to you, and pray for one another with respect to what is shared. You may want to become prayer partners over the matter, men with men, women with women.

THOUGHT FOR THE WEEK

It is always good and spiritually renewing to stop and remember what God has done for you by sending His Son to earth in order to save you. It is healthy to remember what you were before and to contrast that with the change that has taken place by the washing of regeneration—

rebirth—and by the renewing that comes by the rich out-pouring of God's Holy Spirit in your life. What you lost through Adam's sin, you regain through faith in God's Son—the One who reunites you with the Holy Spirit, whom God once breathed into Adam and Eve.

If you have believed on the Lord Jesus Christ and are a true child of God in the common faith, if you are God's own possession, then your life is to be one distinguished by good deeds—good deeds that will glorify your Father who is in heaven and His Son who is coming soon to reign as King of kings, good deeds you will someday find very profitable. As Revelation 22:12 says, He is coming soon, and His reward is with Him to give to every man according to his deeds.

Jesus saves you, and it is all pure grace. But you determine your reward by the way you appropriate that grace and live in its full measure. May God's grace toward you not be in vain. May you labor in the grace of God until you see the face of God and hear His "well done."

Theme of Titus:

SEGMENT
DIVISIONS

		PARAGRAPH THEMES	CHAPTER THEMES	*Author:*
		1:1-4		*Historical Setting:*
		1:5-9		*Purpose:*
				Key Words:
		1:10-16		
		2:1-15		
		3:1-11		
		3:12-15		

NOTES

1 Timothy

1. KJV; NKJV: *doctrine*
   ESV: *doctrine, teaching(s)*
2. NIV: *command*
   KJV; NKJV: *commandment*
   ESV: *charge, learn*
3. ESV; NIV; KJV; NKJV: *sound doctrine*
4. ESV; NIV; KJV; NKJV: *learn*
5. KJV; NKJV: *bishop*
6. NIV; KJV: also *deacon*
7. NIV: *good teaching*
   ESV; KJV; NKJV: *good doctrine*
8. NIV: also *these matters, them* (in verses 15,16)
   KJV; NKJV: also *them* (in verses 15,16)
   ESV: also *them, this* (in verses 15,16)
9. NIV: also *doctrine*
   KJV; NKJV: *doctrine*
10. ESV; NIV: *teaching*
11. NIV: also *godly*
12. NIV: *teaching*
    ESV: also *teaching*
13. NIV: *sound instruction*
    KJV; NKJV: *wholesome words*
14. NIV: also *to worship God*
    ESV: also *godly*

2 Timothy

1. NIV: *testify about our Lord*
   ESV: *testimony about our Lord*
2. NIV: *And of this gospel*
   KJV: *Whereunto*
   NKJV: *to which*

3. NIV: *That is why*
    KJV: *For the which cause*
    ESV: *which is why*

4. NIV: *the pattern of sound teaching*
    KJV: *the form of sound words*
    NKJV: *the pattern of sound words*
    ESV: *the pattern of the sound words*

5. ESV; NIV: *good deposit*
    KJV; NKJV: *good thing*

6. NIV: *remember (recalling, reminded, remind)*
    KJV: *remembrance (mindful, call to remembrance, put thee in remem-brance)*
    NKJV: *remember (mindful, call to remembrance, remind)*
    ESV: also *reminded*

7. KJV: *afflictions (suffer, chain)*
    NKJV: *sufferings (suffer, chain)*

8. NIV: *deserted*

9. NIV; NKJV: *endure hardship*
    KJV: *endure hardness*
    ESV: *share in suffering, suffering*

10. NIV; NKJV: *chained*
    ESV; KJV: *bound*

11. NIV: *to the point of being chained*
    KJV: *unto bonds*
    NKJV: *to the point of chains*
    ESV: *bound with chains*

12. NIV: *wandered away*
    KJV: *erred*
    NKJV: *strayed*
    ESV: *swerved*

13. NIV: *the things you have heard me say*
    KJV: *the things that thou hast heard of me*
    NKJV: *the things that you have heard from me*
    ESV: *what you have heard from me*

14. ESV; NIV: no equivalent word used
    KJV: *the same*

15. NIV: *God's word*

16. KJV: *Wherein*

17. ESV; NIV; KJV; NKJV: *Therefore*

18. KJV; NKJV: *afflictions*
19. KJV; NKJV: *suffer persecution*
20. KJV; NKJV: *my doctrine*
21. ESV; NIV: *what*
22. NIV; KJV; NKJV: *holy Scriptures*
23. ESV; NIV: *message*
    KJV; NKJV: *words*
24. ESV; NIV; NKJV: *message*
    KJV: *preaching*
25. KJV; NKJV: *afflictions*
    ESV: *suffering*

Titus

1. NIV: *actions, doing*
   KJV; NKJV: also *work(s)*
   ESV: *work(s)*
2. NIV: *doing, wickedness*
   KJV: *works, iniquity*
   NKJV: also *works*
   ESV: *works, lawlessness*
3. NIV: *teaching*
   ESV: also *teaching*
4. ESV; NIV: *self-controlled*
   KJV; NKJV: *sober-minded*
5. KJV; NKJV: *soberly*
   ESV: *self-controlled*
6. ESV; NIV: *self-controlled*
   KJV: *sober*
   NKJV: *sober-minded*
7. NIV: *things, doing*
   KJV; NKJV: *works*
   ESV: *work(s)*
8. KJV: *Holy Ghost*

Notes for Personal Study

NOTES FOR PERSONAL STUDY

NOTES FOR PERSONAL STUDY

Notes for Personal Study

NOTES FOR PERSONAL STUDY

NOTES FOR PERSONAL STUDY

*D*o you want a life that thrives?

Wherever you are on your spiritual journey, there is a way to discover Truth for yourself so you can find the abundant life in Christ.

Kay Arthur, David Lawson, and Bob Vereen invite you to join them on the ultimate journey. Learn to live life God's way by knowing Him through His Word.

Visit www.precept.org/thrives to take the next step by downloading a free study tool.

PRECEPT
MINISTRIES
INTERNATIONAL
THE INDUCTIVE BIBLE STUDY PEOPLE

Books in the
New Inductive Study Series

❧❧❧❧

Teach Me Your Ways
GENESIS, EXODUS,
LEVITICUS, NUMBERS, DEUTERONOMY

*Choosing Victory,
Overcoming Defeat*
JOSHUA, JUDGES, RUTH

Desiring God's Own Heart
1 & 2 SAMUEL, 1 CHRONICLES

Walking Faithfully with God
1 & 2 KINGS, 2 CHRONICLES

*Overcoming Fear
and Discouragement*
EZRA, NEHEMIAH, ESTHER

*Trusting God
in Times of Adversity*
JOB

*Praising God Through
Prayer and Worship*
PSALMS

*God's Answers for
Today's Problems*
PROVERBS

*Walking with God
in Every Season*
ECCLESIASTES, SONG OF SOLOMON,
LAMENTATIONS

Face-to-Face with a Holy God
ISAIAH

Listening to God in Difficult Times
JEREMIAH

What Is Yet to Come
EZEKIEL

*God's Blueprint
for Bible Prophecy*
DANIEL

*Discovering the God
of Second Chances*
JONAH, JOEL, AMOS, OBADIAH

*Finding Hope
When Life Seems Dark*
HOSEA, MICAH, NAHUM,
HABAKKUK, ZEPHANIAH

*Opening the Windows
of Blessing*
HAGGAI, ZECHARIAH, MALACHI

The Coming of God's Kingdom
MATTHEW

Experiencing the Miracles of Jesus
MARK

The Call to Follow Jesus
LUKE

*The God Who Cares
and Knows You*
JOHN

*The Holy Spirit
Unleashed in You*
ACTS

*Experiencing the
Life-Changing Power of Faith*
ROMANS

*God's Answers for
Relationships and Passions*
1 & 2 CORINTHIANS

*Free from Bondage
God's Way*
GALATIANS, EPHESIANS

That I May Know Him
PHILIPPIANS, COLOSSIANS

*Standing Firm in
These Last Days*
1 & 2 THESSALONIANS

*Walking in Power,
Love, and Discipline*
1 & 2 TIMOTHY, TITUS

The Key to Living by Faith
HEBREWS

*Living with Discernment
in the End Times*
1 & 2 PETER, JUDE

God's Love Alive in You
1, 2, & 3 JOHN,
PHILEMON, JAMES

Behold, Jesus Is Coming!
REVELATION

Harvest House Books by Kay Arthur

Discover the Bible for Yourself
God, Are You There?
God, Help Me Experience More of You
God, How Can I Live?
How to Study Your Bible
Israel, My Beloved
Just a Moment with You, God
Lord, Help Me Grow Spiritually Strong in 28 Days
Lord, Teach Me to Pray in 28 Days
Lord, Teach Me to Study the Bible in 28 Days
A Marriage Without Regrets
A Marriage Without Regrets Study Guide
Powerful Moments with God
Speak to My Heart, God
With an Everlasting Love
Youniquely Woman (with Emilie Barnes and Donna Otto)

Bibles
The New Inductive Study Bible (NASB)

Discover 4 Yourself® Inductive Bible Studies for Kids

God, What's Your Name?
How to Study Your Bible for Kids
Lord, Teach Me to Pray for Kids
God's Amazing Creation (Genesis 1–2)
Digging Up the Past (Genesis 3–11)
Abraham—God's Brave Explorer (Genesis 11–25)
Extreme Adventures with God (Isaac, Esau, and Jacob)
Joseph—God's Superhero (Genesis 37–50)
You're a Brave Man, Daniel! (Daniel 1–6)
Fast-Forward to the Future (Daniel 7–12)
Wrong Way, Jonah! (Jonah)
Jesus in the Spotlight (John 1–11)
Jesus—Awesome Power, Awesome Love (John 11–16)
Jesus—To Eternity and Beyond! (John 17–21)
Becoming God's Champion (2 Timothy)
Boy, Have I Got Problems! (James)
Bible Prophecy for Kids (Revelation 1–7)
A Sneak Peek into the Future (Revelation 8–22)

NOW AVAILABLE IN
NASB® & ESV®

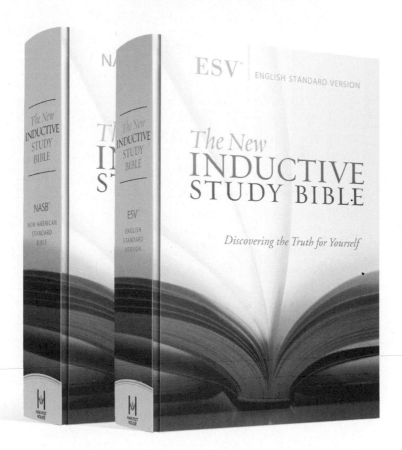

The Gold Medallion–winning *New Inductive Study Bible* (over 700,000 sold) is now available in the trusted English Standard Version. This Bible is based entirely on the inductive study approach, leading readers directly back to the source and allowing God's Word to become its own commentary.

Also available in Milano Softone™ and Genuine Leather!

For more information, visit www.precept.org/store.
Make sure to check out Inductive Bible Study Training opportunities!

DIGGING DEEPER

Books in the New Inductive Study Series are survey courses. If you want to do a more in-depth study of a particular book of the Bible, we suggest that you do a Precept Upon Precept Bible Study Course on that book. The Precept studies require approximately five hours of personal study a week. You may obtain more information on these powerful courses by contacting Precept Ministries International at 800-763-8280, visiting our website at www.precept.org, or filling out and mailing the response card in the back of this book.

If you desire to expand and sharpen your skills, you would really benefit by attending a Precept Ministries Institute of Training. The Institutes are conducted throughout the United States, Canada, and in a number of other countries. Class lengths vary from one to five days, depending on the course you are interested in. For more information on the Precept Ministries Institute of Training, call Precept Ministries.